teach yourself

blogging

nat mcbride

jamie cason

D0542131

for over 60 years, more than 50
million people have learnt over 750
subjects the **teach yourself** way,
with impressive results.

be where you want to be
with **teach yourself**

For UK order enquiries: please contact Bookpoint Ltd, 130 Milton Park, Abingdon, Oxon OX14 4SB. Telephone: +44 (0)1235 827720. Fax: +44 (0)1235 400454. Lines are open 09.00–17.00, Monday to Saturday, with a 24-hour message answering service. Details about our titles and how to order are available at www.teachyourself.co.uk.

For USA order enquiries: please contact McGraw-Hill Customer Services, PO Box 545, Blacklick, OH 43004-0545, USA. Telephone: 1-800-722-4726. Fax: 1-614-755-5645.

For Canada order enquiries: please contact McGraw-Hill Ryerson Ltd, 300 Water St, Whitby, Ontario L1N 9B6, Canada. Telephone: 905 430 5000. Fax: 905 430 5020.

Long renowned as the authoritative source for self-guided learning – with more than 50 million copies sold worldwide – the **teach yourself** series includes over 500 titles in the fields of languages, crafts, hobbies, business, computing and education.

British Library Cataloguing in Publication Data: a catalogue record for this title is available from The British Library.

Library of Congress Catalog Card Number: on file.

First published in UK 2006 by Hodder Education, 338 Euston Road, London, NW1 3BH.

First published in US 2006 by Contemporary Books, a Division of the McGraw-Hill Companies, 1 Prudential Plaza, 130 East Randolph Street, Chicago, IL 60601, USA.

The **teach yourself** name is a registered trademark of Hodder Headline.

Typeset by MacDesign, Southampton

Printed in Great Britain for Hodder Education, a division of Hodder Headline, 338 Euston Road, London NW1 3BH, by Cox & Wyman Ltd, Reading, Berkshire.

Hodder Headline's policy is to use papers that are natural, renewable and recyclable products and made from wood grown in sustainable forests. The logging and manufacturing processes are expected to conform to the environmental regulations of the country of origin.

Impression number   10 9 8 7 6 5 4 3 2 1

Year   2010 2009 2008 2007 2006

v

contents

contents

preface

If you're reading this, you are – or someone you know is – probably thinking about starting up a weblog. You think you probably ought to be out there on the Internet, writing about the stuff you know and care about. You think that people will probably want to hear what you've got to say. You know what? You're probably right!

People sometimes think blogging is just about keeping an online diary. Sometimes that's true, and it can be interesting – some people can set out the minutiae of everyday life in a novel way. But most blogs are much more than that. They are invaluable sources of information about niche subjects, or handy guides to other interesting websites. They are wide-ranging conversations between many people; they are trusty friends where you know you'll find a good joke on a Monday morning ...

Blogs are as varied as the bloggers who blog them, and that's where their beauty lies – because *anyone* can be a blogger. In the bad old days if you had something to say, you had to throw money into printing and distributing a magazine. Now you can open up your thoughts to the world without spending a single penny. You need no special equipment or technical knowledge: just you, your computer ... and maybe a book like this.

This book will explain what blogs are, how they work, and how to choose the right kind of blog for you. It gives step-by-step instructions to get it up and running, to add photos, links and multimedia clips. It explains legal and editorial issues you should be aware of, and how your blog can earn you money. We assume no prior knowledge of website coding or management, and only minimal experience of using computers and the

Internet. However, we do also include a section on advanced techniques for those readers who like to get their hands dirty with the underlying technology.

There are about 50 million weblogs out there on the Internet – go on, make it 50 million and one!

Nat McBride & Jamie Cason

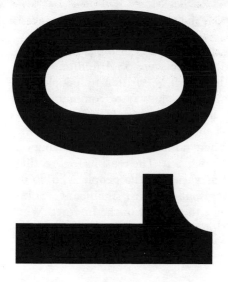

01

introduction

In this chapter you will learn:

- about where and how the blogging phenomenon arose

- how blogging may develop in the future

- what a blog really is and why you might want one

1.1 A brief history of weblogs

In 1996 there were no recognized weblogs or blogs. By the end of 2005 it was estimated that there were 53.4 million hosted weblogs. The majority of these will be written by people like you, people who need to find a simple way of communicating on the Internet. You are only a few steps away from being one of them. Sometimes these people may be publishing personal views, expert opinion, pictures of their family or simply reflecting on their observations of life as they live it. The reasons for creating and maintaining a blog are as varied as the people who do it. Collectively, their efforts represent the most significant revolution in democratic media since the advent of the Internet. Who invented them? What is a blog? Why would you want to have one for yourself?

In the beginning

Like most phenomena associated with computing, the popularity and diversity of blogs and blogging has risen exponentially with the affordability and connectedness of computers. But its origins are quite specific and can be credited to a few talented programmers who wanted to add their voices to the Internet publishing platform of the World Wide Web.

The bloggers

At the time of writing (early 2006), Google has indexed over 8 billion pages of information on the Internet. Which ones are worth reading? Initially, weblogs were conceived as logs of pages that a particular author or editor had visited and found interesting. The term was first coined in 1997 by Jorn Barger (http://www.robotwisdom.com). The early bloggers recognized that it would be helpful to have someone editing or pre-surfing all that web content. Weblogs were a way of sorting the wheat from the chaff. For them, their friends and colleagues it was a way of sharing information they regarded as important. The act of weblogging added value to the sites that had been chosen. Their relevance had been affirmed by someone whose judgement was trusted.

PETERME.COM

Links, thoughts, and essays from Peter Merholz.

« February 2006 | Main | April 2006 »

March 31, 2006

ASTORIA, OR - THE GOOD AND THE BAD

Last night, we stayed in Astoria, OR, after a day of driving from Seattle.

Washington proved a little disappointing to me -- we didn't have the time to head north up the Olympic peninsula, so we headed due West to Aberdeen and then Long Beach, which were just not all that interesting. Though Long Beach did have a killer pinball arcade.

We continued south and found nothing worth stopping at until we got to Astoria. We ate at Gunderson's Cannery Cafe, where I got an excellent Manhattan, and a tasty order of Laksloda -- a Scandinavian preparation of salmon and potatoes. Oh, and the desserts, a berry cobbler and a Pavlova, were divine.

We stayed at a delightful little motel, the Crest, the was dog-friendly (and didn't charge extra for pets!).

We tried to get breakfast at a popular spot in town, the Pig 'n Pancake, but the quality of the coffee and food was *so bad* we couldn't eat it. Avoid at all costs.

TRAVELS

See Me Travel

ARCHIVES

April 2006
March 2006
February 2006
January 2006
December 2005
November 2005
October 2005
September 2005
August 2005
July 2005
June 2005

Peter Merholz's blog at www.peterme.com

As early bloggers started to recognize each other, find each other's sites and make links to them from their own, Peter Merholz playfully developed the term as a verb, as in 'we blog', to describe what this emerging community were doing. Thus blogging was born. The early weblogs tended to be written by people who worked on the Internet and understood how to create web pages from scratch. By 1999 a number of tools were released which meant the technical barrier to publishing a weblog was removed. The appearance of Pitas (www.pitas.com) and PyraLabs' Blogger (www.blogger.com), saw an explosion in the number of blogs. Creating and updating a weblog was as simple as typing text into a box on a webpage.

The nature of weblogs changed as they started to be used as a platform for personal publishing, as much as a filter for other web pages. Content was as varied in size, shape and kind as their authors. Apart from personal diaries, bloggers have used the form to analyse and critique mainstream news stories and media, publish expert opinion on topics in which they specialize, as a soap box for their political views and as a place for essays about the quirky, lovable behaviour of their pets – particularly cats.

Pitas (www.pitas.com) was one of the first sites to offer blogging facilities

1.2 What is a blog?

There are four attributes which are commonly agreed to define a weblog.

- A weblog is a webpage which consists of chunks of text called posts which are regularly added.

- Each post has a date of entry. Posts are presented in reverse chronological order, that is, the most recent is at the top.

- The content of the weblog may 'filter' other webpages by presenting links to them with the weblog author's comments.

- The content of the weblog may be a journal of the author's thoughts, feelings or observations.

The first two points are fairly simple structural things to notice about the organization and maintenance of information in weblogs. The second two cover the very broad spectrum of possible uses of a weblog and are a simplified way of describing how weblogs have been used.

Why would I want one?

A weblog can be anything that you want it to be. Blogging is about giving you a voice. If you're reading this book it is likely that you might be interested in publishing a weblog or are already doing so. To give yourself a foundation for many years of happy and successful blogging, you should develop a clear vision for your weblog. Try answering these questions:

Do you often come across other web pages which you think are relevant, witty, interesting? Do you find obscure pages off the beaten track which deserve a wider audience? If you do, you might want to follow in the footsteps of the first bloggers and create a filter style blog with links to these pages annotated with your pithy comments.

Are there subjects which you follow closely or are particularly expert in? This could be professional or amateur interest. The topic may be something to do with work or a hobby. It could be a public issue about which you feel strongly. The world needs to hear your thoughts on these matters.

Cameron Barrett's Camworld is one of the longest established blogs

Do you enjoy writing? Or rather, do you want to get into writing or improve, but don't have a reason to write at the moment? Blogging can be an excellent tool and discipline to get you turning your thoughts into coherent points. Because you'll be writing regularly, you will definitely see an improvement in your self-expression over time.

Do you look for yourself in Google and find nothing? Unless you share a name with someone famous, the chances are that if you publish a weblog, you'll quickly become the top result for your name in Google (unless you use a pseudonym of course!). Just think of all the old friends and colleagues who are wondering how you're doing now, but are coming up with lists of people who aren't you when they google. They are your audience, they're waiting for you to perform.

How much time can you spare for blogging? You may have to invest some time which you currently spend on something else. You should consider how much time you're prepared to allocate and try and plan your blogging into a daily, weekly or monthly

<u>Weblog Archive</u> > <u>2006</u> > <u>April</u> > <u>13</u>   <u>Previous/Next</u>

▤ **Thursday, April 13, 2006**   **Last update**: Thursday, April 13, 2006 at 3:52 PM Eastern.

Pretty soon Google is going to have a feature that Teoma has had for a while. I think they're almost there, in fact. When you search for a <u>term</u> that has more than one meaning, it will present all the possible meanings as top-level items. Each will have a wedge next to it. Click on the wedge to expand or collapse all hits related to that meaning. That way if you're searching for Bull Mancuso, you won't have to consider hits related to the body parts shop in Syracuse, NY; or the restaurant in Peekskill. It's possible that this can extend into a multi-level hierarchy and can be prioritized by who you are. Suppose your uncle is named Bull Mancuso. Seems

<u>Dave Winer</u> ✉

 Search

<u>Comment on today's
Scripting News</u>

Community Directory

Dave Winer's Scripting News

routine. A blog that is updated in fits and starts may struggle to retain readers. A blog not updated at all is a dead blog. If read at all, it will elicit, at best a sigh of sympathy and at worst create the impression that you are a person who is guilty of wanton neglect of their webchild.

Things to avoid

You should consider carefully before publishing inflammatory comment about work, friends and family. Never say anything in a blog that you aren't prepared to say to someone's face or say to a room full of people including that person. It will come back to haunt you. People have been sacked for defaming their employers online.

Without wanting to stifle your self-expression with political correctness, try and avoid racist, homophobic or sexist comment. Remember that what can sound reasonable in your head, might sound obnoxious in public and will cause all but racists, homophobes and sexists to shun you.

And, obviously, don't publish your name, address, details of your home security and times you're likely to be out of the house.

There'll be more on the legal pitfalls of publishing in Chapter 4.

1.3 Blogging today

Blogs are firmly established as the simplest method for the average person of finding their voice on the Internet. The phenomenon has had a massive impact in the way traditional media businesses source and publish information on the Internet. It has redefined the importance of the individual voice in relationship to big media and has forced the media industry to re-evaluate the importance of individuals, as experts, commentators and eye-witnesses. At time of writing, in 2006, blogging has become mainstream. The number and diversity of sites continues to grow, the early bloggers and the tools they created have developed into businesses, often merging or being acquired by bigger online players, and being offered to their larger subscriber bases. For instance, Blogger is now part of Google.

There are a number of more established, hosted services – Radio Userland, Typepad, LiveJournal and new entrants in the market such as MSN Spaces. News services offer blogs as part of their portfolio, most notably the BBC (Search BBC News for "BBC Blogs" http://tinyurl.com/bm524) and *The Guardian* (http://blogs.guardian.co.uk/news). Whoever they are, online publishers are likely to be implementing blogging-related technology like the RSS standard for syndication as a way of reaching readers. There are hundreds of pieces of software out there to help you organize and track the blogs you like to read (http://en.wikipedia.org/wiki/List_of_news_aggregators) and others are adopting these tools as people become used to consuming blogs as part of their daily information intake.

The future of blogging

It is likely that blogging will continue to grow in diversity and scope. While they won't replace news journalism, blogs, blogging technology and format will become essential parts of the media mix. Tools to keep abreast of your favourite blogs will be integrated into your web browser and computer desktop. Using them will be the equivalent of adding a page to your Favorites. Our children will grow up with the ability to create blogs and an expectation that their voices have value. While not everyone will blog, those that do will increasingly be able to add richer content to their sites such as pictures, sound and video. Ultimately, blogging will become so absorbed by the mainstream that it will no longer be worthy of separate comment and we won't need to write or buy books about blogging!

1.4   Further reading

Blood, Rebecca. *Weblogs: A History and Perspective*, Rebecca's Pocket, www.rebeccablood.net/essays/weblog_history.html

Barrett, Cameron. *Anatomy of a Weblog*, 1999, www.camworld.com/archives/001177.html

Sullivan, Andrew. *The Blogging Revolution*, Wired 2002, www.wired.com/wired/archive/10.05/mustread.html

The Blogging Geyser, Perseus, www.perseus.com/blogsurvey/geyser.html.

Summary

- Blogging is a new phenomenon which is growing rapidly – and is here to stay.

- A weblog or 'blog' is a website where (usually) small chunks of text are posted regularly and arranged in date order.

- A blog may consist of annotated links to other useful websites, or standalone original content.

- It is a way for readers to get a handle on the billions of web pages on the Internet …

- … and for writers to publish their work quickly and easily.

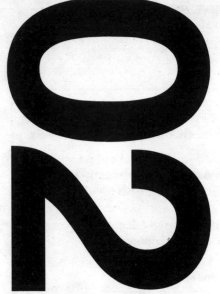

02

start before you

In this chapter you will learn:

- how to work out who and what your blog is for
- how often you will update it
- what you will need from it
- how to choose a provider

2.1 Who and what is your blog for?

It is worth taking some time to think through a few key aspects of your weblog before you start. While it's tempting and so darned easy to jump right in, an investment now will pay dividends in the future when your initial enthusiasm is starting to abate, other things in your life demand your weblogging time or you realize that the feature set of the weblog service provider you rejected is actually the one you should be using.

First up, ask yourself some basic questions about what and who your blog is for. The more closely you can identify the purpose of your weblog and its audience in your own mind, the easier it will be to write and create content for it. The 'what is it for?' and 'who is it for?' are closely interrelated. It might be easier to start with identifying what your blog is for. Is it a personal diary, an encyclopaedia of your comments on other websites, a corporate site for work, school or club? Is it a specialist commentary on an aspect of science or TV science fiction? Is it a series of poetic musings on life or a place to rant about the latest computer game that's rocking your world?

At the same time kick around ideas for a title for your blog. Once you're done, nail this title and purpose or tag line in a simple sentence. Like this 'St Margaret's School Weblog – the definitive guide to life, work and play at this Idaho elementary'. Or if it's a personal piece 'John Doe Does – the online diary of an everyday guy'. Maybe the title is more abstract and wacky like 'A Little 'Otter – Bespoke bed-warmers and water bottles'.

You're creating a trademark or brand for your site. Ideally this will be memorable, catchy and help visitors understand what to expect from your site. It is also worth checking if you can get this name to carry through somehow in your URL. (What that is and how you deal with it in practice are covered in Chapter 6.)

If the purpose of the weblog is shared with other people, either through an organization like a school, workplace or club, or as a collaboration with friends, make sure you've identified all the people that need to agree the purpose and title, and that they understand that they share this responsibility, and plan time with them to discuss ideas and a date to sign-off on a decision.

Boing Boing – www.boingboing.net. A self-styled 'directory of wonderful things', Boing Boing is the archetypal blogzine, created by a group of talented writers

Gourmet Club – http://blog.americanculinaryacademy.com/ SignOnSanDiego.com's Gourmet Club have used the power of the weblog to present themselves online

The kind of topics that your weblog might cover include family, friends, TV, news, sport, technology, media, games, school, work – the list is endless. It is probably worth thinking about some subdivisions of these broad categories too. For instance, it might be that you want to create content about your school or work. And when you think about school or work, you might realize that they tend to be made up of projects or products, colleagues or co-students, bosses and teachers, events and contexts like the local community or a marketplace of competitors.

The more you can break down these topics, the more tuned up your weblogging senses will be. It will be easier to spot content opportunities when examples arise in real life, as links you find on the Web or as content on TV or in the press. Your relationship with your readers, viewers and listeners should be as instinctive as your everyday interactions with your mother, spouse, friends or work colleagues. Conversely, if you're looking for an outlet for the hidden 'you', the one your nearest and dearest don't normally see or hear, try and imagine that sympathetic confidante that just gets what you're on about. Have fun with it. Spend some time giving this fantasy reader a name, a history, a life. At the very least, this exercise will flex your imagination and creativity.

Whether your ideal audience is real or imagined, try and identify what it is about your style that people appreciate. Are you witty, humorous or plain speaking? Do you notice little things that

Grumpy Gamer – www.grumpygamer.com – Renowned developer, Ron Gilbert takes an unashamedly curmudgeonly view in his games industry-watching blog

others miss? Do you have an elephantine memory? Do you obsess over topics? Do you like an old-fashioned, no-holds-barred rant about issues that concern you? Ask people who you trust and who know you well for some pointers about what it is about you that might play well in an opinionated, informative or amusing weblog. Remember that the kinds of traits that might make you a persistent and successful weblogger don't necessarily have to be positive!

It can be hard to be objective about yourself, and you may find this process daunting. Another way of approaching this task is to try and analyse the media you enjoy. Do you look at anyone else's weblog? What is it about their site that you like, that makes you come back for more? What about TV, radio, films, videogames, books, newspapers and periodicals? What is it about the shows and movies you like, the writers you read, the games you play? Really try and be specific and objective about this analysis and make a point of making as many written notes and lists of things as possible. It's important that it is written down because then it becomes material you can start to work with it, not just a fleeting, uncaptured thought. Give yourself a period of time to really start observing your habits and preferences. You'll discover that this skill of detaching yourself, observing and reflecting will come in handy later as your weblogging career develops.

When you're noting down the list of weblogs you like and read regularly, make sure you get the URL links down too, as these sites will be some of the first content you publish on your own site and will go on to define your relationship to the wider weblogging community.

At the end of this process you should have:

+ A title and a tagline
+ A list of topics and sub-topics that you intend to cover
+ A list of 'values' that define your style
+ A list of other sites like yours.

If you don't have all these things or you're not happy with them, go back over them once more. Remember they don't have to be perfect or finished, but must exist in some form as they will be the foundations upon which you build your blog.

2.2 How often will you update it?

This is a key question and one which you'll need to give some serious thought. There's no such thing as a non-updated weblog, only dead websites which no one visits. Or to put it another way, you're only as good as your last post. On the brighter side, a post can be as short or as long as you (or your audience) prefer, and can be good, bad or indifferent. Over time, the quality level will, inevitably, rise, but you shouldn't worry about that too much. The quality will look after itself; your only responsibility is to get something posted, relatively frequently. As a rule of thumb: a post a day keeps the weblog doctor away. But weekly or fortnightly might make more sense to your schedule or the frequency of news on your topic.

The crucial thing is to set your update schedule and make sure that you stick to it. This is a solemn pact between you and your audience. Stick to it, deliver on their expectation that you're still

Civic Minded – www.civicminded.corante.com – a group blog about the impact of the Internet on politics and advocacy

there, still having thoughts, opinions, experiences, observations and you'll start to build a following. By all means over-deliver from time to time. A few bonus posts never go amiss. And feel free to change your schedule, going more or less frequent, but just make sure you let your visitors know where they stand. Sometimes having a site where the responsibility to post is shared with others can be really helpful. It's good to share the load, as you can cover vacations and absence due to sickness or lack of inspiration! Working in a group can also help you set deadlines for each other. Take these seriously and treat your fellow editors with respect. Again, be honest about how much or little you can do with yourself and them.

You may need to audit the other things that currently occupy your time, especially if you already find there are not enough hours in the day for all your responsibilities and interests. You might need to negotiate with family, friends or colleagues in order to get their support. You may have to bargain with them for a slug of time that you would have spent together, which is now devoted to your worldwide audience!

But be specific: how much time do you really need? A solid hour a day? Or week or fortnight? If you're like a lot of bloggers, you'll start to find that your blogging glands begin to work in the background all the time. A chunk of your brain will turn into a weblog casserole, a cook pot of thoughts and posts-in-progress. To support this you could get into the habit of making little notes, *aide-mémoires* as French bloggers say. Always carry a pen. Leave pen and paper in places around your house for when inspiration strikes. In which case, you'll need only a short time to compose and post something that has being brewing in your notes.

If you're hunting down web content, make some focused time to dig up some web treasure. Maybe in a lunch-hour? Maybe after the kids have gone to bed? Or after your parents have? Start by making time to read other people's weblogs, primarily the ones you link to, as this is guaranteed to kick up something you can comment on or add too. As long as you've chosen dedicated bloggers to populate your blogroll, you'll be part of a virtuous circle of content creators who inspire and encourage each other with their efforts.

Blogroll

Blogroll is both a generic term for 'those weblogs which you link to' – by convention presented on the right-hand side of the page – and an online service to help you manage the publication of those links. Find it at www.blogroll.com.

2.3 What will you need from it?

Up to now we've been looking at what others might get from your site. But it's worth remembering what you want to achieve from the site. Before you start take some time to set some targets. These will be the measures of success, enabling you to reflect on your efforts as your site grows and develops. These can be the measures that enable you to assess whether the blog is worth the amount of time and money you might be investing. Apart from a target number of posts per month, one of the primary targets is numbers of visitors or traffic. This has several aspects. There are the number of people who visit, the number who comment, the number of other sites that link to yours. Have a think about what you'd like to achieve in these metrics. Be realistic though,

Traffic measurement page in TypePad

as traffic takes time to build and will be directly proportionate to the amount of effort you put into the site and to raising awareness of it, otherwise known as marketing.

If your work is of a high standard or your views are special enough, you may find someone who wants to hire you to blog or to contribute to some other site, magazine or channel.

It is possible to accept advertising on your site. There are more details on how to do that in Chapter 11. Remember, the likely income of your site from advertisers is related to the number and kind of visitors to it. Your income is usually dependent on how many times your visitors click on the advertising links that your site carries.

If you're blogging for work or school there may be a number of objectives derived from the corporate needs of your organization. Maybe a number of sales leads or enquiries, perhaps an increase in profile or awareness in a community or market, or even just ranking in popular search engines like Google.

There are also softer targets. Blogging involves a lot of content creation, usually writing but perhaps also video and audio making. Are your pieces improving? Is your style becoming more 'true' the more you do? Which posts are you really proud of? Which ones are benchmarks for you to try and better in the future? You'll probably be increasing, in some way, your knowledge and insight into the design and technology of websites. If these are areas that interest you, perhaps you could make a point of adding or researching new features for your site. Make a note of new or confusing jargon or technology references and make a point of searching for more information. Even if you think you'll never need to use it, gradually you'll become better informed and will start to see how different sites deploy different kinds of technology to provide different kinds of experiences and services.

The design of a site is important. It affects how easy it is to use, how pleasing it is to look at and how it reflects on you or your organization. Most of the major hosted services provide a number of tried and tested templates which do a great job of making a usable site and making you look pretty professional. But you may want to start to experiment with designs, perhaps inspired by other sites you've visited. You may find yourself haunting some of the web design specialist blogs and sites. Once you start thinking about design and how people use things, you'll find yourself looking at everything with a new and critical eye!

2.4   Choosing a provider

Now you're ready to make a decision about how your new site is going to be hosted and what tools or software you'll need to keep it updated. The first thing you'll need to decide on is: are you going to host the weblog on your own server or do you want to use one of the hosted services that are available? The first option may be the one for you if you already run a web server or you want to go deeper into the technology that powers the Internet. It's beyond the scope of this book to help you to set up a server, but Chapter 6 will guide you through the process of renting webspace from a provider and using it to host your blog.

And of course it is still possible to publish your site by hand-coding webpages in HTML to emulate the weblog format – but we're assuming that you'll be interested in one of the software packages offered by the mainstream providers. Even experienced coders have opted for the ease of use and the low-cost, hassle-freedom of using a service like TypePad, Blogger, UserLandRadio, LiveJournal or Xanga.

The more detailed the groundwork you've done, the easier it will be to make a choice as to how best to get your new site on to the Internet. There are some questions that you should be able to answer, which will equip you to make the best choice.

Service provider checklist

♦   How much do you want to spend? There are lots of services out there that let you get started for free, especially Blogger (www.blogger.com). But the more features you want, the more you'll have to pay. Payment is usually structured as an annual subscription.

♦   How many contributors, people permitted to post, will your site have? Typepad (www.typepad.com) has powerful features for enabling a number of primary contributors.

- How much traffic do you think you'll get? It's likely that this will be relatively small in the first instance. Compare the bandwidth allowances of different services to see how their offers differ.

- What kind of content will you be uploading? Do you want to be able to view more than just text? Check out the facilities for storing and viewing pictures, playing back or downloading audio or video 'podcasts'.

Podcasts

Podcasting, a combination of Apple's 'iPod' and 'broadcasting', is a method of allowing users to subscribe to a feed, and to receive new, largely audio, files by automatic download. The idea being, you can stick 'em on your MP3 player and listen whenever and wherever you want, unlike normal broadcast radio. More in Chapter 9.

- How much storage space will you need? Is it just text? Are you uploading 700Mb movies? Check out how much server space the provider is letting you have.

- Ease of update – most systems follow a process of completing fields in a web form. If you can, try some out to see how they feel. How easy is it to include a link, a picture? How easy is it to go back and edit a post, or to reassign its category?

- Customizability – how much control do you get over the look of your site? Can you edit the basic templates as your skills grow?

- Are you happy with a subdomain URL for your site, e.g. www.yourblogname.typepad.com or do you want your own special domain name e.g. www.nameofyourblog.com? Does your service support this? Is it clear how they'll help you get this set up? See Chapter 6 for more on this.

- One of the great things that sets blogging apart from other forms of media is that it is conversational. Most services will enable you to allow comments from your visitors on your posts. Check out how much control you have. You may want to disable that feature or only allow it on certain posts. There is another downside too – there are so-called comment spammers who will post thinly disguised boosts

Service	Blogger	TypePad Basic	TypePad Plus	TypePad Pro	Blogware	WordPress	Expression Engine
Comments	Yes	Yes	Yes	Yes	Yes	Yes	Yes
Categories	No	Yes	Yes	Yes	Yes	Yes	Yes
Trackbacks	No	Yes	Yes	Yes	Yes	Yes	Yes
Pings	No	Yes	Yes	Yes	Yes	Yes	Yes
RSS/Atom	Atom	Both	Both	Both	Both	Both	Both
Blogroll/Lists	No	Yes	Yes	Yes	Yes	No	No
No. of blogs	No limit	1	3	No limit	1	1	No limit
Moblogging	Yes	Yes	Yes	Yes	Yes	Yes	Yes
Photo Galleries	No	Yes	Yes	Yes	No	Yes	Yes
Spam Fighting Tools							
Blacklist	No	Yes	Yes	Yes	Yes	Yes	Yes
Visitor registration/login	Yes	No	No	No	Yes	Yes	Yes
Moderation	No	No	No	No	No	Yes	Yes
Comment notification	Yes	Yes	Yes	Yes	Yes	Yes	Yes
Interface & admin							
Templates	33	6	6	6	23	7	27
Multiple authors	Yes	No	No	Yes	Yes	Yes	Yes
Image/file uploading	Image	Both	Both	Both	Both	Both	Both
Password protection	No	Yes	Yes	Yes	Yes	Yes	Yes

Blogging Service Provider comparison Ease of update

for their own sites as comments on your posts. What does your prospective provider have to say about tools to help you eradicate comment spam on your site?

- Syndication – most services will support what are known as RSS or RSS Feeds (see Chapter 9), and these may not be important to you at first, but are powerful tools for retaining an audience as they allow users to subscribe to your blog and are essential for podcasting.

Who's your daddy?

Most blogging services have grown from garage start-ups and are now owned by bigger organizations. Go with Blogger and you're making a deal with Google, sign up with MySpace and you're on News International Corporation's books, and MSNSpaces speaks for itself. Take the time to make sure you're happy with the corporate papa of the service you choose.

Summary

- Take the time to lay the foundations of your blog – decide who and what it is for.

- Note down a title and tag line which sum up the blog, and decide on the topics and sub-topics it will cover.

- Make lists of the values your blog will embody, and of similar websites you like.

- Decide how often you can update it and stick to a schedule.

- Compare blogging services – and where possible, make use of free trials – before settling on one.

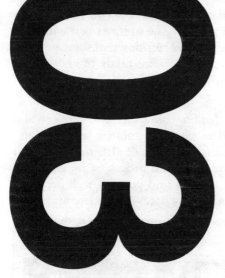

03 get blogging!

In this chapter you will learn:

- how to create a new account with two popular blog services

- how to set up and design your blog with either service

- basic skills for working with text and images in your posts

- how to publish your first post

3.1 Signing up for an account

In the last chapter you worked out what it is you want from a blog, and what you will be able to give to it. Armed with that deep self-knowledge, and our handy run-down of some popular blog services currently available, you are ready to choose one and get blogging.

Throughout this book we'll be illustrating the ins and outs of blogging using two of the leading blog services, Blogger and TypePad. If you've decided to go with another service, don't worry – the rest of the book is not wasted! Other services will differ in detail, but the basic ideas and processes are generally the same. Read on and you should find yourself well prepared for riding the road to blogstardom, whatever vehicle you choose.

Blogger – www.blogger.com

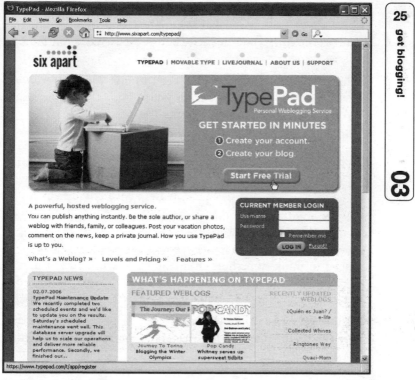

TypePad – www.sixapart.com/typepad

The first thing you will need to do with any service is to sign up for an account from which to run your blog – or blogs, plural, if you are fast of finger and have too much to say for one blog alone. This is usually pretty simple and the sign-up process will generally move you straight on to some basic set-up tasks for your blog.

Sign-up checklist

Here's a checklist of useful information to have to hand when signing up:

* Username and password – it sounds silly, but don't you just hate getting to that bit on a form unprepared, so you have to think up some login details you know you're going to forget 43 seconds after hitting the Submit button...?

- Security question and answer – if you forget your password (see above), you may need to supply a security question and answer to prove your identity before a password reminder is issued.

- Screen name – you may also need to give a *nom de plume* which is used to sign off from your posts. This is the name your readers will know you by.

- Blog name.

- Blog description or tag line.

- Preferred URL for your blog – in Chapter 6 we will look at giving your blog its own domain name (e.g. www.*myblog*.com). But you may be given the option to customize the URL (web address) to some extent. For instance, with Blogger, you can have *myblog*.blogspot.com. So you will need to think of a shortish, memorable word to put here – see the box opposite, on **Domains and subdomains** for more on this.

- Photo or image for your profile – you don't have to have one of these, but it's nice for readers to be able to hang your words onto something visual. You're not applying for a passport though, so it doesn't have to be a straight face-to-camera image if you don't want to do that. Be creative, find something which suits the tone and content of your blog: a grainy police mug-shot, a cityscape, an abstract logo or a totem animal. Use a photo of your pet cat if you really must.

- Your list of 'values' and other sites you like – these will be useful when choosing a design template.

You won't need all of these for every blog service, and you can change your blog's name, tag line and design whenever you like. But you'll need a bit of discipline to get the best out of blogging, so try to start as you mean to go on – be prepared before you take to the stage, and treat your audience with respect. Even if to begin with your audience is Population: 1 – just you.

Domains and subdomains

When you look at a web address (or 'URL'), the bit between the **http://www.** and the first slash (/) is called the **domain name**. For instance, TypePad can be found at **http://www.sixapart.com/typepad** so the domain name is **sixapart.com**

All webpages have to have an address which includes a domain name. When you sign up for a blog, its address will have to use the provider's domain name unless you have bought your own domain name and arranged for your blog to use that address (more on this in Chapter 6).

You may be allowed to choose a **subdomain**, which is the bit which comes between the **http://** and the domain name. For instance, when Nat signed up with Blogger he chose the subdomain 'stupideconomy' so his blog is at **http://stupideconomy.blogspot.com**

Note that any part of a domain name, even a subdomain, can only consist of letters, numbers and hyphens. And try not to make it too hard to remember – keep it simple!

3.2 Signing up with Blogger

1 To create an account with Blogger, go to the website at www.blogger.com and hit the **Create your blog now** button.

2 On the next screen, enter your username, password, display name and email address (Screen 1 on the next page).

3 Click the **Continue** button to move on to the next screen, where you will give your blog a name and a customized URL. You are also asked to type in a sequence of letters and numbers shown on the screen as a distorted image. This is to prevent unscrupulous people from using programs to automatically sign up for blogs, thus gaining free webspace for their dodgy content (Screen 2 on the next page).

4 Click **Continue** to move on to the next screen, where you will choose a design template. You can change the template at any time later on, and in Chapter 7 we will also look at

Creating an account at Blogger: screens 1 (top) and 2 (bottom)

customizing the templates further, or creating your own from scratch. But choose one for now, using your list of values and sites that you like, to help decide which best suits your blog.

5 Blogger will prepare the structure and webspace for your blog.

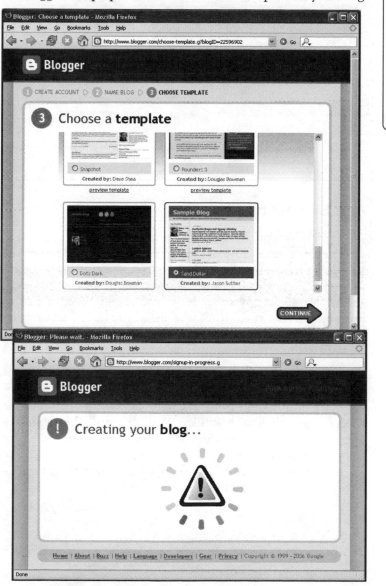

6 In a few seconds it will be ready – click **Start posting** to blog away!

Your Blogger profile

The content of your blog is the primary reason anyone would want to visit and read it, but Blogger is keen on the idea of 'the person behind the words', and it gives you the tools to maintain a personal page. Readers who like your blog can visit this page to find out about any other blogs you might have, or just to know more about you. How much detail you leave is entirely up to your own instinct for fame or anonymity. In addition to some standard personal information, you can list your favourite movies and music or answer a wacky random question just to show what a good sport you are.

Summary information from this page can be dropped into the pages of your blog, with a link to the full profile. The standard page templates include a section at the top for your profile, which shows your screen name and an optional image, and a link to the full profile. When we look at customizing templates in Chapter 7 you will find out how to add to this.

3.3 Signing up with TypePad

1 To create an account with TypePad, go to the website at www.sixapart.com/typepad and click on the **Free Trial** link.

2 On the next screen, enter the details you are asked for. You *cannot* change your subdomain once you've signed up, so make sure you're happy with it before you continue. If not, give it some more thought and come back and sign up later.

3 Click the **Continue** button to move on to the next step – designing your blog. On this screen, choose a name for the blog (you *can* change this later if necessary!).

4 Choose a suitable **layout structure.** Think about what kind of content you have planned for your blog – will it be mainly text or pictures? Does it revolve more around a theme or a timeline? Will you have lists of links as well as posts?

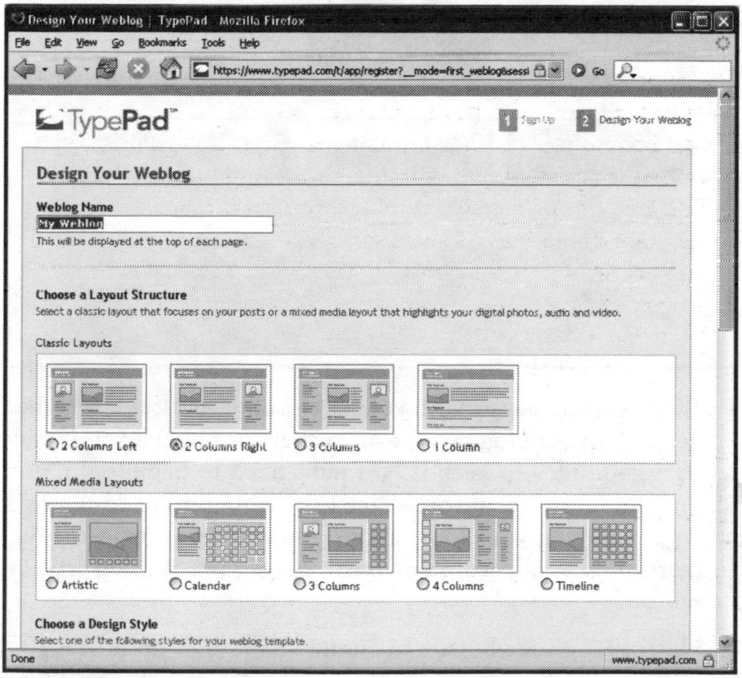

5 Scroll down to the **design style** section. TypePad's ready-made templates are organized into collections of similar designs –

use the drop-down **Show:** menu to select **Bold Palettes**, **Classic** designs or **Special Interest**, for instance. When you change the selection, a new set of templates is shown in the box beneath. Have a look through and choose one you like. We will find out how to tinker with the design in Chapter 7 later, so don't worry if you don't find anything which is absolutely perfect.

6 When you are happy with your design choices, decide whether you want your blog open to all viewers or not just yet. It may be a good idea to keep it **Not publicized** to begin with, just until you have spent some time getting used to making posts and managing your blog. But if you can't wait to get it out there, then by all means go for it! Choose your **Weblog privacy** option.

7 Hit the **Continue** button to complete the sign-up process.

3.4 Overview of Blogger and TypePad interfaces

OK, now you have your blog – it's almost time to wow the world with whatever it is you plan to wow it with – your first pearl of wisdom or pithy slice of wicked wit, the scene-setter for your factual or fictional diary, or an introduction to your collection of holiday/family/cute cat photos. But let's just have a quick tour of your new home on the Web first.

The Blogger interface

When you log into your Blogger account you will start off at your 'dashboard'. This gives you access to your blog(s) and your personal profile, plus links to Blogger's own news, help and

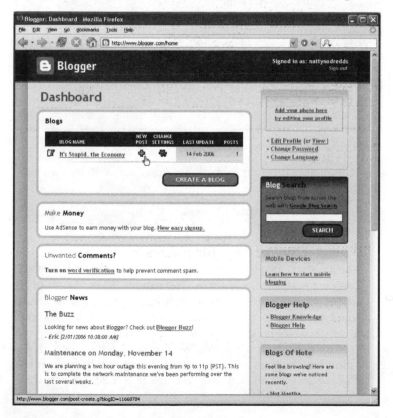

featured blogs. You can return to this page at any time by clicking the Blogger logo at the top left of the screen.

Click on a blog's name for access to all your admin features – writing and editing posts, configuring design templates or settings for sharing or restricting access, managing paid advertising, and so on.

Editing your blog's settings at Blogger

The admin area has four tabbed sections, each with its own sub-menu of options:

* **Posting** – write and edit here; work with unpublished drafts and published posts.

* **Settings** – the default settings are perfect for getting you started, but as you become more sophisticated in your blogging you can adjust them. You can set the way your posts are formatted, published and archived; control the extent to which readers can add comments to your posts; control access by any co-bloggers; link your blog and email together; and manage content syndication. We'll come back to these in the following chapters – for now, just have a quick look at the **Basic** settings. This is where to come if you decide you want

to rename your blog or update the tag line: make your changes, then scroll down and hit the **Save Settings** button.

- **Template** – choose a new design template here, or edit the current one (see Chapter 7 for more on this). If you sign up to have paying advertising on your blog, this is where you control how and where ads are placed.

- **View Blog** – this opens your blog in a new window.

The TypePad interface

When you log into your TypePad account, you are taken to your homepage – this has links to your blogs, photo albums and other TypePad features, as well as to TypePad news, help and useful information. You can return to this page at any time by clicking the TypePad logo at the top left of the screen. As you visit other screens while working with your TypePad account, you will see a list of links appear beneath this logo. These links are called a

Editing the design at TypePad

crumbtrail and are designed for easy navigation through the screens.

One of the advantages of a paid service such as TypePad is that you get more than just a basic blog. TypePad gives you online photo albums too, and a feature called TypeLists, which is a way of organizing links to your favourite people, music, books, or websites and reusing them on more than one blog. These extra features mean that the TypePad interface is slightly more complex. At the top right of the page, you have four tabs for managing the main sections of your account, each of which has a tabbed sub-menu with relevant options.

• **Weblogs** – lists your blog(s); click on a blog name to open it and work with the design options and basic settings, or to create and manage your posts.

• **Photo Albums** – create and manage photo albums to store your pictures online.

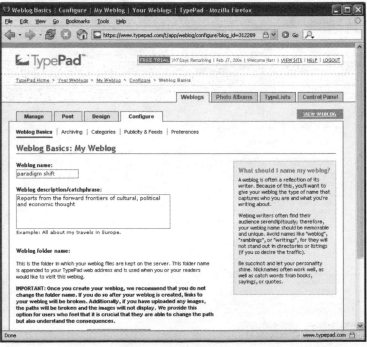

Changing your basic blog set-up in TypePad

- **TypeLists** – create and manage lists of favourite things, which can be used on multiple blogs without having to update them separately each time.

- **Control Panel** – configure more advanced settings for your blogs, view usage statistics, manage file uploads, and (if you have signed up for a premium package) options for earning advertising revenue.

3.5 Posting with Blogger

1   Log in and hit the **New Post** link on your dashboard next to your blog's name, or if you are already working on the blog, click the **Posting** tab.

2   This takes you to the Create Post page, which consists mainly of a text window with a toolbar for formatting text and adding pictures and links. These tools enable you to build posts rich in style and substance without having to understand any

webpage coding. If you *do* know some HTML, you'll also notice that you can hit the **Edit HTML** tab at the top right of the window and dive right in. Otherwise, stay in **Compose** mode and use the toolbar to work with the content of your post.

3   You'll notice that at the bottom of the page there are two buttons – **Save as Draft** and **Publish Post**. So if you run out of time and haven't finished your post – or you get cold feet about publishing it at all and want some time to reflect! – you can save your work and come back to it later. This is also useful when you know you're going to be too busy to compose whole new posts for a while – you can rack up a few drafts in advance and then just quickly log on and publish them from time to time.

4   You might want to save all your posts as drafts to begin with so that you can spend some time getting to grips with the interface before going live.

5   To begin: type a title into the **Title** field. Now tap away in the main text window to write your post and hit **Publish Post** when you're done. If you clicked the **View Blog** link near the top of the page, you would now see your post out – it's out there on the Internet already!

Tip

Even if you *do* know your way around HTML, it's probably best to stick to the toolbar for handling the formatting, links and pictures, for two reasons. First, it's easier, quicker and less prone to typos than hand-coding. Second, Blogger will mark up the code using fully compliant style tags. This is not only better in abstract technical terms, but it is important in practice that text is marked up correctly when your blog is converted into XML format for feeds (see Chapter 9).

Managing your drafts and published posts

When you sign into your Blogger account, if you click on the name of your blog you will be taken to a list of your posts. By default, this lists the five most recent posts, both draft and published, but you can adjust these settings using the drop-down filters. There is also a search box so that you can look up old posts containing matching search terms.

3.6 Posting with TypePad

1 Log in and choose the blog you want to add a post to (if you have more than one).

2 Hit the **Create a Post** link on the panel on the right of the screen, or if you are already working on the blog, click the **Post** tab. This takes you to the create post page, which consists mainly of a text window with a toolbar for formatting text and adding pictures, files and links. These tools enable you to build posts rich in style and substance without having to understand any webpage coding. If you *do* know some HTML, you'll also notice that you can hit the **Edit HTML** tab at the top right of the window and dive right in. Otherwise, stay in **Compose Post** mode and use the toolbar to work with the content of your post.

3 Type a **Title** for this post into the field above the main text window, and then select a **Category** if you want to file this

post in a particular section of your blog. You can use any of the popular categories suggested in the drop-down list, or create your own: just select **Add a new category** and type a name for it in the pop-up window.

4 Type the body of your post into the main text window and hit the **Save** button when you're done. It's as simple as that – your post is now published and publicly accessible (depending on the privacy settings you chose for the blog when setting it up).

You'll notice there are some other options beneath the main text window. The first one, **Posting status**, is used to decide whether to publish the post immediately, or to save it as a draft for the moment. You can also select a future publishing date, so that you can rack up a few posts in advance of taking a holiday, and have TypePad publish them at regular intervals to keep your hungry readership happy. To do this, choose the **Publish on ...** option from the drop-down menu and then pick a date from the calendar in the pop-up window.

Tip: save often!

Remember: blogging is a web-based activity, and unless you are sending your posts from a mobile phone or by email (see Chapter 7), you have to be online and logged in to be composing a post. If you temporarily lose your Internet connection (it happens sometimes, even with a good fast connection), you could lose any unsaved content. It's pretty annoying to spend an hour crafting a finely-tooled piece of wordsmithery only to see it disappear in a puff of binary smoke, so do yourself a favour and save your work frequently in draft form!

3.7 Formatting text in your posts

So creating a post is pretty easy, right? Good. But let's look at some of the features Blogger and TypePad give you for working with the appearance of your content. Your post will already be formatted according to the design template you chose – but you can adjust the style of different bits of text to emphasize them as required.

To format text, click one of the buttons described on the next page and start typing – or select a chunk of text you've already written and then hit the button.

Blogger	TypePad	Description
Courier	N/A	Choose a font face
Small	Normal	Choose a font size
T	A	Choose a font colour
b	B	Make text bold
i	I	Make text italic
N/A	U	Underline text
N/A	S	Mark text with a strike-through
≡	N/A	Left-align text (default)
≡	N/A	Centre-align text
≡	N/A	Right-align text
≡	N/A	Justify text
≔	≔	Numbered list
≔	≔	Bulleted list
66	+66	Start blockquote*
N/A	99+	End blockquote, return to normal
⌀	N/A	Remove all formatting (set it back to the page default)

* Blockquote indents text at both sides and styles to indicate that you are quoting from somewhere.

NOTE: even in Blogger you have no formatting options on the title. The style of all post titles is set as part of the page template and can't be changed from one post to the next.

To see how your post is going to look when it's live on the blog, click **Preview**. In Blogger, this is a link at the top right of the main text window; in TypePad it is a button at the bottom of the screen. Click **Hide Preview** (Blogger) or **Re-edit this post** (TypePad) to return to edit mode and continue writing.

Keyboard shortcuts in Blogger

To make it even easier to work with text, Blogger givers you some handy keyboard shortcuts in the post editing window.

[Ctrl] + [B]	bold
[Ctrl] + [I]	italic
[Ctrl] + [Z]	undo
[Ctrl] + [Y]	redo
[Ctrl] + [Shift] + [A]	make hyperlink
[Ctrl] + [Shift] + [P]	toggle preview/edit mode
[Ctrl] + [Shift] + [S]	publish post
[Ctrl] + [Shift] + [D]	save as draft

Other features – pictures, links, spelling

You'll notice some other buttons on the editing toolbar in both TypePad and Blogger:

Blogger	TypePad	Description
		Add picture (see Chapter 5).
N/A		Upload file (see Chapter 5).
		Make hyperlink (see Chapter 4).
N/A		Make email hyperlink (see Chapter 4).
		Click this to spellcheck the entire post.

When you run a spellcheck, any non-dictionary words will pop up in a small window with suggested alternatives. To help decide what you want to do, the word is shown in context in the box to the right.

Weirdly, 'blogger' isn't in Blogger's dictionary…

You can **Replace** or **Ignore** just this instance of the unrecognized word, or you can **Replace All** or **Ignore All** instances in the whole post. Alternatively, if you know the word is OK, if it's an unrecognized proper name, or if it's just a made-up word you plan to use again, you can tell Blogger to **Learn** it. Then next time you run a spellcheck it won't bother you about this one.

3.8 Pop-up windows

In this age of spam advertising, most browsers now offer some kind of pop-up blocking security. This stops you getting inundated with ads for porn sites, ring tones and useless software, but unfortunately it also interferes with the normal workings of some sites! If you don't see anything happening when you try to use the spellchecker, it's probably because the pop-up has been blocked.

Look at the top of the browser window for a notice informing you that a pop-up was blocked. The appearance and location of this notice varies from browser to browser, and depends also on any additional web toolbars installed, such as Google or Yahoo!

This is the Firefox notice:

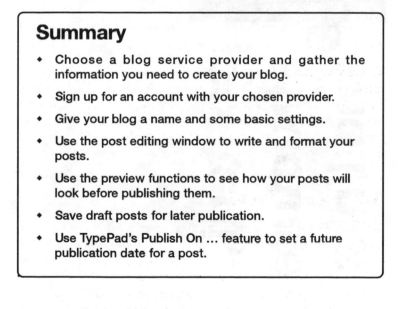

Somewhere, you will find the notice, and there will be an option there to allow pop-ups from the current site. Make sure that typepad.com or blogger.com are on the blocker's 'allowed' list and try the spellchecker again.

Summary

- ◆ Choose a blog service provider and gather the information you need to create your blog.

- ◆ Sign up for an account with your chosen provider.

- ◆ Give your blog a name and some basic settings.

- ◆ Use the post editing window to write and format your posts.

- ◆ Use the preview functions to see how your posts will look before publishing them.

- ◆ Save draft posts for later publication.

- ◆ Use TypePad's Publish On ... feature to set a future publication date for a post.

04

content, structure and links

In this chapter you will learn:

- how to write for the Web
- about the law as it can apply to blogs
- how to organize your blog
- what to do about links

4.1 Writing for the Web

There are some common guidelines to any form of written English and then some specific things to consider when writing for your blog. Here are ten hot tips. These tips are offered as a guide only. The main thing is to write something and then write another thing. Keep repeating this pattern and your writing will get better!

1   Avoid unnecessary words. Every word costs your reader a little bit of time and a little bit of energy. Save their time and energy!

2   Keep sentences short and punchy. Avoid elaborate sub-clauses. Not only will your posts be easier to read, they'll have more impact. And you won't sound like a Dickensian lawyer.

3   Chunk it up! Written content on the Web works best in brief chunks or paragraphs of no more than three or four sentences. It is easier for the eye to scan a screen of chunks and easier to consume them. Blogs, being made up of formatted posts, tend naturally to chunk.

4   Pep up your titles. These are the most important words in your post as they help to build interest and encourage the reader to find out more. Like tabloid headlines, the best post titles will sum up the content, may create a witty (or cringe-worthy) pun and will hook your reader. Spend a couple of minutes more on the title, maybe even write it last.

5   Avoid jargon, or at least remember, that not everyone has the same reference points as you. As your readership grows you'll need to be sensitive to any in-jokes, specialist language or jargon. Take the extra time to explain a reference, or make a link to a source which will help as a glossary or context to your terms.

6   Define your style. It might be a good exercise, especially if writing with others, to define a common style. You might want a very informal feel or a very precise tone. Professional publications will have a style guide covering everything from the italicization of movie names to a list of banned clichés. Often these can be found online and might be worth a read.

7 Avoid clichés. Phrases such as 'at the end of the day', 'to be fair' and 'bet your bottom dollar' should only be used ironically – they have no other value. And you'll invent your own clichés. Just watch out for them!

8 Write like you speak, but without the hesitation, repetition and cliché.

9 Re-read before posting – maybe twice – and at least make sure the meaning of your post is clear. A second read for spelling mistakes and grammar, if you care about such things, will give your prose polish and increase its credibility.

10 Master convention before breaking with it. But remember that everything's there to be challenged!

These tips are not rules or laws; there is no Internet teacher patrolling with a red pen who'll humiliate you in front of the class. *What* you say will provoke more comment than *how* you say it. And how you say it will usually only provoke comment if it's funny.

And the comment will probably include 'LOL' (Laugh out Loud) or 'ROFL' (Roll on the Floor Laughing). So much for rules! The web, with the possible exception of SMS or texting, has had the greatest impact on how English is written in recent times. These new conventions usually involve brutal short-handing of words,

---

useit.com → Papers and Essays → Writing for the Web   [ ] [Search]

Writing for the Web

Research on **how users read** on the Web and **how authors should write** their Web pages. Mainly based on studies by John Morkes and Jakob Nielsen.

- **Short summary** of the findings: How users read on the Web [read this one first]
- **Full paper** (long): Concise, SCANNABLE, and Objective: How to Write for the Web (unfortunately this paper was written for print and not online)
- **Case study**: Applying Writing Guidelines to Web Pages **improved usability by 159%** when rewriting sample pages from a popular website
- Detailed study materials, including downloadable page files, tasks, and questionnaires (only useful if you want to replicate our experiments or conduct new studies in the area of reading and writing on the Web)

See also these related essays by Jakob Nielsen:

- Low-literacy users exhibit different behaviors
- PR and press releases on corporate websites (75 design guidelines based on usability studies of how journalists visit company sites)
- Email newsletters (scannability even more important than for websites)
- Writing transactional email and confirmation messages
- Teenagers on the Web: poor reading skills and low patience levels mean that text has to be ultra-concise for teens and that more information must be communicated in images
- Tagline Blues: what's the site about?

www.useit.com – Jakob Neilsen's site and content tips

the introduction of special symbols or smileys to convey emotion and the rampant use of slang and technical terms.

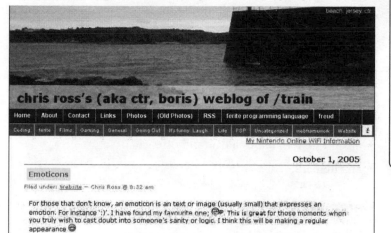

http://www.darkrock.co.uk – UK blogger Chris Ross gives us his take on emoticons

Rich media

While writing is the simplest and easiest form of content creation for your weblog, it is becoming increasingly popular and simple to add other forms of content such as photographs, audio and video. This has become even easier with the integration of cameras in cell phones as most can now support software which enables posting of material straight from your phone to your blog! We'll deal with some of the practicalities of getting yourself set-up to host and post rich media on your site in later chapters.

4.2 The law

When you create a blog you're setting up shop as a publisher, and even though your store of content is probably a very small concern on the global Internet Main Street, it's good to consider some areas of legal constraint on publishers. Law and its application differs from territory to territory and state to state, so these points are intended as a general brief on possible pitfalls you might encounter, as they are areas which most legal systems legislate for. If you think you might rub up against problems with the law it is worth doing more research or seeking professional advice.

The five areas which bloggers might encounter are:

- Defamation and libel
- Copyright
- Privacy
- Adult material and 'harm and offence'
- Incitement.

Defamation and libel

Libel is the recorded form of defamation as opposed to slander which is the verbal form. It is broadly defined as untrue, seemingly factual, statements about a person, persons or organization which would damage their reputation and/or lead reasonable people to shun or avoid them. The key thing here is the ability to justify contentious comments or accusations you make in your blog. Your points need to be based on solid evidence or source material. Reliance on the publication of similar defamatory content elsewhere may not be a defence. Even established publications get it wrong sometimes and pay for their mistakes. The great thing is that personal opinion is fine, as long as it is clear that that is what you're giving. Your opinion that something or someone is great or stinks, or that your feeling that this or that is marvellous or appalling is all classed as fair comment.

Usually the risk of incurring a suit for libel will increase as the readership and the profile of your blog increases. It may be most likely that you run the risk of causing offence to those close to you rather than your more distant corporate or celebrity antagonists. Obviously, your readers are more likely in the first instance to be friends, family and colleagues – the very people who may be the subjects of your posts. The best advice is play nice, even if you don't feel that way. If you must get something off your chest, say it to the person face to face or confide to someone else you can trust. Blogs are terrible ways for blowing-off steam in personal relationships. Remember that the pen (or keyboard) is not known as being mightier than sword for nothing and sometimes a few spoken words or even silence may be more advisable.

Copyright

Copyright is a legal principle which allows content creators to have their literary, artistic and musical work recognized as their property and which protects their exclusive right to make copies of those works and to distribute them. The increasing use of digital technology in the creation and distribution of copyright work is creating all kinds of new cases for copyright lawyers to mull over. Instances of unauthorized use of copyright work are known as infringement. This is a two-way street for the blogger. Bloggers can find themselves both as copyright owners and infringers. You have rights to the material you create as an author and you may incorporate fragments of the work of others in your posts, usually as quotations. In the USA this concept is enshrined in law as 'fair use', but similar defences are not guaranteed in other jurisdictions.

How much of an original work anyone has the right to use is usually a point of debate. The main things to consider are whether the new use builds or expands upon the quoted piece and whether it uses the minimum amount of the original work to make its point. Another factor is commercial. If you make wholesale copies of someone's work, even for an intended fair use, does the use reduce the market for the quoted original by effectively creating a replacement? The best thing to do is to use as little as possible of an original work. If you wish to use the work of others beyond 'fair use' then you should seek approval from those identified as authors or owners of the works you want to use. Displaying fragments of text is one thing, but it becomes a lot harder to justify 'fair use' if you are displaying images, video or music created by another.

Bear in mind also that richer media, like video, is usually a patchwork of rights where writers, performers and composers may all have some rights in the piece. You should always credit authors or content owners, preferably with a link to the original work or a relevant website where possible. Many bloggers take an anything-goes approach to copying and posting content. This is done on the basis that it is unlikely that anyone will object to their infringement, and, if they do, the blogger will simply remove the offending post. However, any lawyers worth their salt would advise 'don't infringe'. Even though the chances of heavy legal retribution are slim, you will save yourself time in the long run by making sure all the material you use is either yours, defensible as fair use or authorized by its owner. That way, you can't go wrong. Plus you may find you make some interesting contacts with your sources and pick up some links from their sites.

Remember, you yourself are now a copyright owner in the original work you publish and you may find your own stuff subject to infringement. Before calling your lawyer, do consider all the points above. Is the new use 'fair'? Can you negotiate with the infringer directly to either take down or modify their use so that you are satisfied? If they won't play ball, can you complain to their Internet service provider or blog hosting service? Most corporate entities will try to avoid infringement and are likely to be sympathetic to genuine claims. Do consider very carefully if it is worth getting really serious with your infringer through the courts. It will cost a good deal of time and money, and a negotiated settlement is always likely to be your best bet.

Lessig.com – Lawrence Lessig is a leading Internet copyright theorist and activist and founder of the Creative Commons movement

Another good piece of news is that there is a certain amount of material out there which is either free of copyright or rights are readily available for certain uses. There are conventions that you can use to indicate to people that you are happy to allow certain uses of your work. The leading movement in this area is the Creative Commons which is a really straightforward way of managing your rights and understanding the rights of others. The organization has pioneered declarations of rights which are really easy for both humans and computers to understand, without the aid of lawyers.

Privacy

When you're publishing your weblog you need to be aware of issues of privacy both for you and the people you may post about. You should avoid publishing previously undisclosed private facts about individuals, unless you can justify a public interest or 'newsworthiness' in that information becoming public. I'm sure you can imagine the kind of sensitive issues that can arise around sexuality, financial position or commercial or trade secrets. Often these kinds of facts are held to be private until the person concerned chooses to disclose or publish them. Imagine how you would feel if someone 'outed' you as a homosexual before you were ready to tell, or if they published your bank statement in the newspaper.

Publication of these kinds of facts can be defended legally where a legitimate public interest can be demonstrated. It might be legitimate to 'out' you as a homosexual, if you were engaged in a public campaign against gay rights or culture. Your financial position might be a legitimate subject for scrutiny if you were involved in a financial deal or sensitive issue where those facts might be relevant, and you had made public claims which could be proved to be false. There are separate issues about how private information is obtained. The interception of mail and electronic communication, including telephone, is specifically legislated for in most jurisdictions so consider carefully whether wiretapping or email server hacking is a good content supply strategy for your site!

People have some rights to physical privacy as well, and the regulations on this are mainly to do with paparazzi intrusion and infringement of the so-called right of 'seclusion'. In addition to long-lens, tabloid photography and James Bond-style espionage, a simple pitfall to avoid is webcam broadcasting to the Web where those who might be featured are unaware that they are live on the Internet. Similarly, candid-camera type content should usually be cleared with those who are featured. Make sure your subjects are in on the joke and, preferably, in writing!

As observed, privacy is a two-way street. You have rights as a publisher. Many people are concerned to preserve their anonymity or keep secret certain personal details in order to safeguard a right to free speech. Their blogs can be controversial across a range of subjects and could end up having a personal cost for them, in terms of losing current or prospective employment, alienating friends and family. There is statutory protection for free speech in the United States, but still it is possible to post anonymously or use a pseudonym. You can also prevent your site being indexed from search engines like Google, and you can make your site, or parts of it, private, requiring visitors to register and log-in.

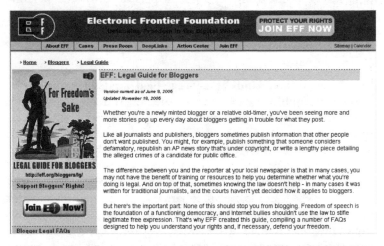

Electronic Frontier Foundation at www.eff.org. Campaigners for freedom of speech on the Internet, the EFF is an invaluable reference for general legal matters

Adult material and 'harm and offence'

If you are intending to publish material suitable for adults then you need to be aware of the laws governing the publication of such material on the Internet. Most territories have some degree of regulation of adult material and usually some community standards for obscenity. Because you are publishing on a global medium you have to be aware of the law where your server is located and those where your content is most likely to be consumed. Child pornography is universally outlawed. If your site is hosted by one of the major blogging services then you should take heed of their regulation on acceptable content.

It is advisable in any case to try and publish advice about any content that you think might not be suitable for a general audience. The idea here is to be as responsible as you can in offering advice and a description about your content, at the point of consumption. Empower your audience with information so they can make a choice as to whether they want to consume your material. Apart from being a common courtesy, this kind of self-policing approach will show you to be a responsible publisher should any kind of dispute arise.

Incitement

If your content features or appears to glorify any kind of extreme behaviour from clips of Jackass TV type stunts to celebrations of suicide or physical violence towards others, you may fall foul of a claim of incitement. That is, encouraging others to imitate this behaviour. That's why TV shows with dangerous physical activities tell you, 'don't try this at home'. But beyond personal misadventure, virtually any kind of criminal activity if depicted or presented in a positive light could be interpreted as incitement on your part. Definitely think carefully about your editorial position on such matters, and the tone you use to approach the subject. Blogs are great for kicking off debate and exchanging views. If you author your content with an open mind, solicit opinion in your comments and try and acknowledge differing points of view. That's just good journalism and your approach to difficult subjects will be highly defensible.

However, you may want to consider the risks of exhorting and depicting direct, illegal action of whatever kind. This is not to say you shouldn't do it: much positive political change has been driven by such activity, but usually at some cost to those brave or foolhardy individuals involved. Remember, one person's freedom fighter is another's terrorist. While in the United States and Britain there is considerable protection for freedom of speech on political issues, you should think very carefully about anything that incites racial discrimination or hatred as this is fairly heavily legislated against in most jurisdictions.

Disclaimer!

This advice is intended as a guide only and will not help you in a court of law. If in doubt seek professional advice or don't press that post button!

4.3 Organizing your blog

One of the joys of blogging is that so much of the organization of your site is based on common conventions, and the software and publishing systems that enable so many blogs handle a lot of the work for you.

For the purposes of organization on screen, there's one thing that holds true for almost all blogs, and is almost a definition of what makes a blog – that is that a blog consists of a series of regular posts in reverse chronological order. Simply that the most recent post appears first. This is handled automatically by blogging software and hosting services. As you make your post, it is automatically marked with the date and time. This information is stored in the descriptive content about your post which is readable by the computer. This kind of machine-readable information is referred to as 'meta content' – content that describes other content. Meta content is often also readable by humans, and one of the most frequently seen elements of meta content are the summaries or titles of pages in search engine results. Because your posts will all have their time and date stamp, you can see that one easy way of dividing up blog content, to make it easier to reference and navigate, is by time. This means that you can call up a page that shows you links to all the posts you made between June and July or all the posts you made in a certain year.

Most systems will also support other ways of categorizing your posts. All you have to do is remember to mark-up or describe the categories that your new post fits into, when you create it. Your system may provide a list of suggested categories and may allow you to set-up your own. These could take the form of descriptive terms such as 'family', 'TV', 'Politics', 'School'. If your post has been marked up with these kinds of descriptors or meta content, then it is easy for the system to find all the posts in that category and display them. These categories are another way of slicing the content by subject as well as by date and time.

As so much of the storage and display of your content is dealt with by the software, you really only need to be aware of what information the system needs you to add in order to make the system work better. The great news is, you don't have to do anything if you don't want to, as the system will always take your stuff and organize it for you.

One thing worth bearing in mind: while the live system will look after your published content, you may want to define a system

See how the posts line up with the most recent at the top

of archiving and back-up for your content. This might be as straightforward as using a process in your blogging software – many offer simple ways of saving all your content back to your hard drive. You may then want to back that copy up to CD or DVD, as we're sure you already do with all your valuable digital data!

4.4 Links

Linking from page to page and site to site is a defining characteristic of the World Wide Web. Blogging culture was built on the idea of links. In the first instance these were links to other sites around the Web, as most of the early blogs consisted of posts which were comments on other websites. This may or may not suit the purpose of your blog, but linking to other relevant material, even if your piece is not necessarily a comment on it, adds value to your post. Just a quick search for any relevant pages out there, as part of your composition process, may yield information that if you find interesting, your audience surely will too. The other linking practice that has fuelled the weblog fire, is adding links to other weblogs that you read and admire. This section is often known as a *blogroll*. This has also become the name of a software product which can help some systems automate the display of this list of links to other blogs.

Doc Searl's, blogrolling at its best, at http://doc.weblogs.com/

Blogroll

Technorati
Doc's podblog
RageBoy/CBO
MysticBourgeoisie
David Weinberger
Dave
Planet Berkman
Memeorandum
John Palfrey
IT Garage
Bret Fausett
Susan Crawford
Bruce Sterling
Syndicate
Sheila Lennon
Don Marti
Wes Felter
Brad DeLong
Brian Oberkirch
Chris Albritton
Ronni Bennett
Kevin Bedell
Howard
Bryan
Deep Fun
BoingBoing
edhat
Terry Heaton
Jay Rosen

Some blogging systems offer special ways of referring to media like books, music and games; which enable you to create lists of work that you like or you desire. You can then lay these out on your page and take advantage of cross-referral systems which will automatically pull-in thumbnail images of the work with links to online retailers.

The importance of including links in your blog cannot be over-stated. By linking to others you will not only provide a service to your readers, but you will raise the profile of your own site. Other site owners will notice if they start to receive referrals from your site and may, in the end, link to you. This is important for the potential for direct traffic to your site. Also, the more sites that link to you, the higher your ranking in search engines which rate the importance of sites according to the number of other sites which link to them. To be part of a web, you need to link and be linked to.

As blogging becomes more popular and the technologies underpinning it become integrated with all kinds of other services, the number of ways of creating cool, automated links to other online content has increased. It is now easy to integrate so-called feeds of content both to and from your site. Linking has never been easier or more important.

Summary

- Writing for the Web, and especially for a blog, is different from writing for print – keep it short and punchy!

- Remember, you can include pictures, audio and video as well as words.

- Read up on the law before stepping into potential legal minefields!

- Try to categorize your posts to make it easier to organize your blog.

- Link, link, link!

05

photos and images

In this chapter you will learn:

- how to add pictures to blog posts
- how to set up a third-party photo storage account
- how to link this into your blog
- other ways to send images to your blog

5.1 A picture is worth a thousand words

So goes the old saying, and it is particularly apt in a web context. Think of the last time you tried reading a thousand words on a webpage. Even with the most sympathetic use of typeface and colour, it's just not very easy on the eye! And you have to think of your readers' time too – most blogs consist of easily digestible, bite-sized entries, because you're expecting your audience to visit regularly. How much time can you really expect your readers to devote to your blog on each visit, if they are visiting once a month, once a week or every day?

If you can condense a lengthy prose description into one nice picture, so much the better. Digital cameras and camera phones are cheap and easy to use these days, and the process of transferring pictures onto your computer is also much more straightforward than it was a few years ago. This part of the process is beyond the scope of this book, so we'll just assume that you've worked out how to get the pictures off your snapper and onto your computer.

Once you've got this far, there are now a number of ways of getting your pics online. You can simply upload the image to your blog along with the text of a new post, using the normal post editor. Or you can set up an online photo album and link the photos into your blog – TypePad offers its own photo album tool, but there are plenty of web-based image sharing services which you can use with Blogger or other blogs. And if you own a camera phone you can also send pictures and text straight to your blog from the phone via MMS.

Using existing web pictures

One way to display a picture on a post is to reference an image which already exists somewhere on the Web. The image will appear on your post with a link back to the original image, wherever that is. This method is good if you already have a stash of images stored elsewhere on the Web. The size and number of pictures featured in your blog is only restricted by the limits of your third-party service, and the process of adding a picture to a post is faster – there is no upload time involved.

Image formats

Pictures can be saved in a number of digital formats for computer use. The most common formats used on the Web are JPEG for photos (JPEG stands for Joint Photographic Experts Group, the working group who developed this industry standard), and GIF for simpler designs, cartoons and animations.

Your camera or phone will almost certainly save its photos as JPEGs – look at the filenames when the pictures are transferred to your computer, they should end in **.jpg**. If this is not the case, you should convert your photos to JPEG format before trying to upload them to the Web – refer to the documentation for your camera or image processing software for how to do this.

You can also do the same thing with other people's pictures from other sites, but there are two reasons why you shouldn't. First, it's actually stealing – not just the intellectual property, but in a very concrete way too. Most webspace providers set limits on the amount of data transferred ('bandwidth') from a site, and will charge site owners for exceeding it, or shut down their site. Whenever someone reads a post which features someone else's picture, the image is sent from that person's website. This uses up some of their bandwidth without giving them the benefit of people actually looking at their site. This is known in the trade as 'bandwidth theft'.

Second, you have no control over the image – the image owner could move or delete it at any time and you'd be none the wiser until someone notices the missing picture.

If you want to use other people's pictures on your site, ask them nicely first and provide a proper credit and link back to their site.

5.2 Adding pictures directly to a post

The easiest way to put a picture on your blog is to add it to a post using your blogging service's picture upload feature. If you're only going to use the occasional image here and there, this is as good a way of handling images as any. A free Blogger account will give you 300Mb of space to store pictures, with a maximum size per picture of 250Kb. That's 1200 good-sized pics at a reasonable print quality, or around 6000 images of web size and quality. The standard TypePad account gives you 500Mb space for all your pictures, posts and other files. The posts themselves take up very little memory, so if you used your space mainly for pictures, you could store up to 2000 good-sized print pics or 10,000 web-sized images!

To add a new picture to a post using Blogger

1 Start a new post and type some text in.

2 Put your cursor where you want your picture to sit and click the Add Image button.

3 This opens up a new window with some image options in it. If you're using an existing web image, enter the URL of the

image into the **Add an image from the web** box on the right of the pop-up window.

4 To find the URL of an image, right-click on it and choose **Properties** – this displays details of the image, including its URL (also called 'Address' or 'Location' by some browsers). From here you can copy and paste.

5 If you are uploading one of your own images, click the **Browse** button next to the box beneath **Add an image from your**

computer, and locate the file you want to upload from your computer.

6 In either case, if you want to add more than one image, click the appropriate **Add another image** link and repeat the process.

7 Now choose the layout you want (if you choose 'none', the picture will be left-aligned, and the text will start again beneath it). The image size determines how big the image appears *in* the post – but Blogger actually uploads a full-size image as well. A link to the full-size image is automatically made so that readers can click on the smaller image to see it in all its glory. When choosing a display size, remember: smaller images load faster, so balance this against visual impact.

8 When you're ready, click **Upload Image** to upload it. This will take a few moments and you'll see the Blogger timer graphic ticking away:

9 When it's finished click **Done** to return to your post-in-progress, which will update itself with the image.

To add a new picture to a post using TypePad

1 In the post editing window, place the cursor where you want the image to be displayed and hit the **Insert image** button. This opens a pop-up window prompting you to browse for the location of the image to be uploaded.

2 If you're happy with the default layout, leave the **Use Default Settings** option selected – this sets the image size at 100 pixels wide, left-aligned on the page; and wraps text to the right, flowing on beneath it.

3 If you'd prefer a different layout, click the **Use Custom Settings** radio button and then set your preferences. If you check the

Save Settings as This Weblog's Defaults, these preferences will be saved and used as the default for all future images added to this blog.

4   When you're done, click **Insert Image** to upload the file and add the image to your post.

5   If you need to move the image around within your post, you can just click and drag it. But remember to check how it looks in Preview mode while you're fine-tuning the positioning: it will be different from the way it looks in the Compose window once the text of your post has been formatted with your page styles.

6   TypePad, perhaps out of respect for the principle of not engaging in bandwidth theft, does not offer a simple way of referencing an existing web image in a post. If you want to add an image without uploading your own copy of it, you will need to edit the HTML directly. This is actually not too hard – see page 102 in Chapter 7 for details of how to add HTML image code. Or pick up a copy of *Teach Yourself HTML* at your local bookstore!

Adding multimedia clips to a post in TypePad

There is a nice feature which allows you to upload other kinds of media files such as audio or video clips. It works in much the same way as adding an image: you hit the Upload file link and browse for the file, then wait while the file is uploaded. TypePad stores the file in your web space and adds a link to it in your post, using the clip filename as the link text.

Storing your photos in a TypePad photo album

TypePad offers its own Photo Album feature which is handy if you plan to use a lot of images in your blog and don't want to go to the trouble of signing up for a third-party service such as Flickr (see page 73). You don't even have to tie it in to the rest of your blog if you don't want to – you could just use it as an easy way to share some photos from a holiday, for instance. If you want to link to an album from your blog, you can – if not, you can treat it as something completely separate.

1   Click on the **Photo Albums** tab to create a new album. In the box on the right of the screen, enter a **name** for the album, then choose a **folder name**. This will form part of the album's web address, so should be short and memorable, containing only letters, numbers and – if absolutely necessary – underscores or hyphens.

2   Decide whether you want this album to be publicly listed by TypePad and then click **Create**.

3   You'll now see a control panel for working with photos in this album, with three tabs:

>   **Manage** – add and delete photos, and give them titles and descriptions.

>   **Design** – choose a layout and style for the album.

>   **Configure** – edit the album's title, description, public/private access, and other settings such as image size and the order photos are displayed in.

4   To add photos to the album, go to the **Manage** tab and click the **Add photos to this Album** link. This opens an uploading page: choose how many images you want to upload in this batch, and then use the **Browse...** buttons next to each box below to locate the files on your computer.

5   A very nifty feature of the TypePad photo album is that it allows you to upload a whole load of images compressed into a single zip file. This simplifies the process of selecting the files, and saves time on the actual upload as well.

6   When you have selected the file(s) for upload, hit the **Upload** button and wait while the files are uploaded and processed.

7   Once your pictures are uploaded you will be taken to the photo listing page, which displays thumbnail images of each photo and summary information. Click on the thumbnail or the title to view or edit its details: here you can change the title or caption, as well as archival information such as where and when the photo was taken. Click **Save and Publish** to save your changes.

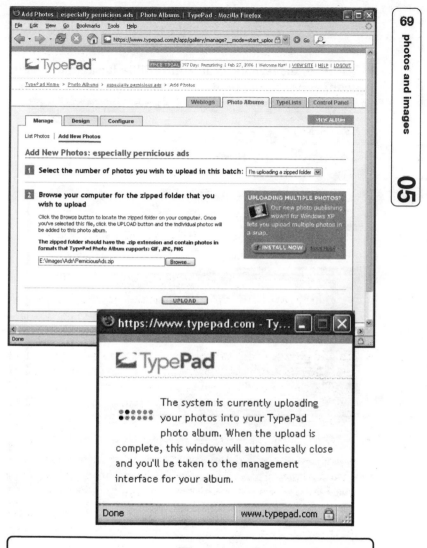

Tip

It's actually slightly quicker to click Save when editing picture titles and captions, but this only stores the settings internally. TypePad won't push the changes through to the album itself (as visible to your audience) until the next time you click Save and Publish.

8 You will probably also want to tinker with the design and layout of your albums. Click the **Design** tab and then work your way through the **Layout, Content** and **Style** options.

9 Start with the layout, because this will influence the content options open to you in the next step.

Uploading batches of images

TypePad has a downloadable photo upload wizard (Windows XP only) which runs from your desktop and handles multiple file uploads in a step-by-step process, thus making life nice and simple. To download and install this, go to the **Photo Albums** tab and follow the link there for download instructions.

Once installed, the wizard integrates with Windows Explorer so that you can browse through your computer's file system, find the pictures you want to upload, and work from there.

Select the files you want to upload and then click **Publish the selected items to the Web** in the **File and Folder Tasks** panel to start the wizard.

Work through the wizard's steps: confirm the files you want to publish, then select TypePad from the list of possible destinations. Enter your username and password, then choose an album for the photos and set resizing options (if you don't want to clutter up your storage space with massive full-size image files). When all files are uploaded, click the **Finish** button and visit your album – you should find that all the new photos have been neatly inserted as thumbnails with links to the bigger images.

You will still need to log into your TypePad account and edit these via the photo album manager if you want proper titles and

Web Publishing Wizard

Where do you want to publish these files?

Select a service provider to host your Web site. If you do not have a membership account, one will be created for you.

S̲ervice providers:

MSN Groups
Share your files with others, or store them for your personal use.

TypePad
Personal Weblogging Service

< B̲ack   N̲ext >   Cancel

Web Publishing Wizard

Do you want to adjust picture sizes before publishing?

The wizard can resize your pictures so that they transfer faster and are easier to view by the recipient. These adjustments do not affect a picture's proportions. Also, smaller pictures will not be adjusted.

Do you want to resize these pictures?

☑ Y̲es, make them all this size:

○ S̲mall (fits in a 640 by 480 window)
◉ M̲edium (fits in a 800 by 600 window)
○ L̲arge (fits in a 1024 by 768 window)

< B̲ack   N̲ext >   Cancel

Working through the Web Publishing Wizard

captions – but at least getting the files up onto the Web from your computer was quick and easy.

Linking photo albums to your blog

Each photo album you create (as long as you have marked it for public access, not private) can be included in your blog. Click on the **Weblogs** tab to open the blog manager and then click **Design** on the tabbed sub-menu. In the central box, click the **Change Content Selections** link: this takes you to a page listing all the different bits and pieces which comprise your blog template. About halfway down on the right hand side, you will see your photo albums listed – tick the one(s) you want to include and then click the **Save** button at the bottom of the page. The album title and most recent photo will now appear in the sidebar, with a link to the front page of the album.

Unfortunately, TypePad does not offer an easy way of adding a single image from your photo albums to a post on your blog, so here are two ways of getting around the problem. The non-technical way is to just upload the photo as part of the post, as described above. This duplicates the storage, because the image is saved once to your album and then again to your blog – but as we've estimated you've got room for at least 10,000 web-quality images, this is probably nothing to worry about!

The alternative is to edit the HTML code for the post and add a small piece of image code to it. If you are familiar with HTML already, just get the URL of the image from your album, then open the posting screen and code away in the **Edit HTML** view. If you're not an expert web coder (why should you be?), see page 102 in Chapter 7 for instructions.

5.3 Photos on a third-party service

There are a number of great services for storing, organizing and sharing your photos online, such as Fotki, Buzznet, PhotoBucket, PhotoLightning and more. Many of these also offer easy ways to post your pictures to a blog. We'll just look at one popular service as an example of how this works – Flickr. A free account with Flickr gives you unlimited storage, although there are some restrictions on how many photos you can add each month. You can also upgrade to a paid service which has more generous terms.

But first, why would you want to go to the trouble of setting up another account to store photos when you have plenty of space on your blog anyway? The reason is that a specialist photo service offers a lot more than just storage space. You will be able to organize your photos into albums, and add captions, descriptions and keywords, making it easy for you and other viewers to search through your pictures. If you have a lot of pictures online, this ability to organize and search quickly becomes very useful indeed.

You can still use the pictures on your blog, and it's really no more work than uploading them directly with a post, once you've gone to the trouble of signing up for a photo service. In fact, Flickr has a little program you can download and install on your computer which allows you to upload a whole batch of photos at once, which is even easier than adding them to your blog one at a time. And in addition to having the pictures blogged in a specific context, you've also got them neatly filed away if you ever want to find and use them for anything else.

Finally, if those aren't enough reasons, here's one final little bonus – once you've got a Flickr account, you can blog *any* image you find on Flickr, not just your own!

Signing up with Flickr

First, you will need to sign up with Flickr. The service is now owned by Yahoo! – if you already have a Yahoo! ID from using another of their services, you can sign straight into Flickr, just creating a new screen name. If not, signing up for a Flickr account actually means getting a Yahoo! ID and then choosing a Flickr screen name.

1 Go to www.flickr.com and hit the **Sign up!** button. If you have a Yahoo! ID already, sign in with it here, otherwise click on the **Sign up** link beneath the phrase **Don't have a Yahoo! ID?**

2 You'll need to fill in a few details such as name, username, password, security question and answer, and then submit. Once you've got your Yahoo! ID, click the **Continue** button and you're into Flickr.

3 To create an account, you just have to choose a screen name which people viewing your photos will know you by.

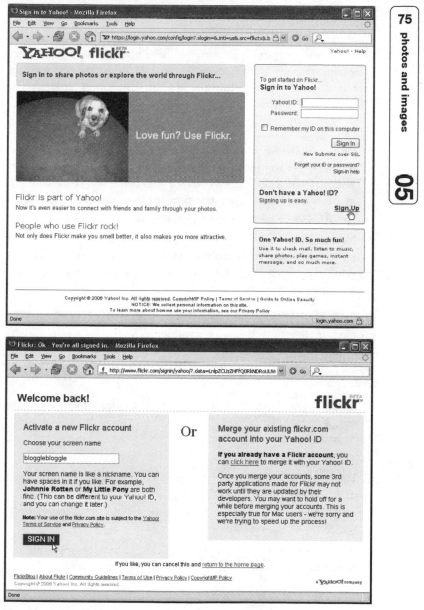

Sign up to Flickr at Yahoo! and activating the account

Uploading images

To start with, let's upload a few photos – I'm assuming you've got some on your computer somewhere you can use. If not, get your camera out right now and take some! What are you waiting for? It doesn't cost anything – get out there and unleash the photographer within!

1 Sign into Flickr and click on the **Upload photos** link.

2 Choose up to six photos from your computer using the **Browse** buttons. Try to upload similar pictures together, because then you can add 'tags' (keywords for searching on) to all of them at the same time. Type the tags into the box as a string of words separated by spaces.

3 You can now choose privacy settings for these pictures – do you want them to be public (available to anyone and every-one), restricted to just friends and/or family, or completely private and visible to you only?

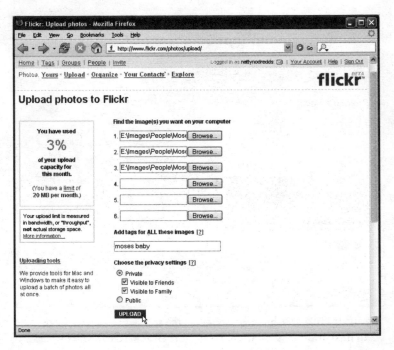

4   Wait until the photos have been uploaded and processed – this will take a little while because Flickr stores each photo in several sizes for different uses.

5   When it's finished you can add titles and descriptions to each photo, edit the tags if necessary and click the **Save** button to complete.

6   Your new photos will be displayed at a small size in a list, most recent first.

7   Click on one to see it at a larger size, with editing options: you can rotate them so they're the right way up, and add notes. This is a nifty little feature – you can highlight an area of an image and attach a short note to it, which viewers can read when they hover their mouse over the highlight.

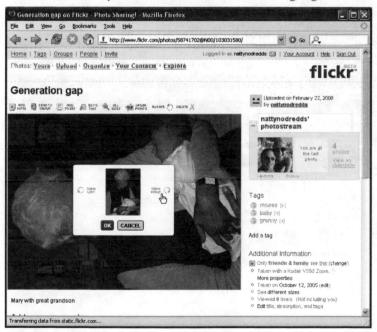

Organizing your photo album

If you're going to have lots of photos, it may help to organize them into albums (called *photo sets* on Flickr). Click the **Organize** link to go to what Flickr, with its strange aversion to the letter 'e', calls the *Organizr*. This is a window with two panels: thumbnails of your photos go in the left panel, and your sets are shown in the right panel.

1   To begin, click the **Load all photos** option in the left panel – once you've built up a collection of photos you will probably only want to work with recently-added ones, so you can use the slider under the panel to show only those photos uploaded between certain dates.

2   When your photos are loaded into the left panel, click the **Create a new set** button in the right panel. Give the set a name and description, then start adding pictures to it.

3   To assign a photo to a set, click and drag the thumbnail across and drop it into the space at the bottom of the right panel.

4   You can also make one of these pictures the *primary photo* of the set – this is a kind of 'cover image'. Click on a photo and drag it into the little square window beneath the description. When you have multiple sets listed in the right panel, this image helps you identify the contents of the set.

5 When you're finished, use the **Yours** link on the navigation menu at the top left of the screen to go back to your pictures.

Uploading by email

You can also upload pictures to Flickr via email. Click on **Your Account** in the navigation links at the top right of the screen, then under **Photo Settings**, click on **Uploading by email**. This will show you your unique email address for uploading images. Type a title for the photo in the subject line of your email, a description in the body, and attach the photo, then just send it to the email address.

5.4 Linking Flickr to your blog

OK, you've got your storage sorted and your photos are all tidily arranged in themed albums with witty captions and helpful search tags. Good for you! But despite all that work, your blog is as dry and image-free as ever. No! Let's fix that. There are two stages to this – first you have to tell Flickr about your blog and how to connect to it, then you just click the **Blog this!** button on a photo to send it straight to your blog as a new post.

To set up the link to your blog, click on **Your Account** in the navigation links at the top right of the screen, then scroll down to the **Blogging** section and click on **Your blogs**.

Click **Set up a new blog** and choose your blog provider from the list. You will be asked to give your blog username and password so that Flickr can post to the blog – but if you're wary of handing out passwords, don't panic. You can leave it blank and then type it in each time you post from Flickr to your blog.

Finally, you need to review the list of blog(s) returned from your account and click **All done** to confirm the details.

Blog this!

Now it's a piece of cake to add a picture post to your blog – just go to your photos and choose a picture. Click on it to view it in its own page, with the image options toolbar above it. In the middle is a **Blog this!** button – click this and then choose a blog from the list to send it to.

On the next page, enter a title for the post and the text, then hit **Post Entry** to send it to your blog. If you chose not to save your password during the set-up process, you'll be prompted to enter it now. And that's it – it's on your blog now!

If you want to adjust the layout for your Flickr-to-blog posts, go to the **Your blogs** page and click the **Layout** link. This gives you a few layout options to choose from – pick one and click the **Use This** button to save it. If you're familiar with HTML and CSS you can further **Customize** the layout.

Summary

+ Use the **Add picture** button to include images in your posts.

+ Upload your own images where possible: ask before linking to images on someone else's site.

+ Store and organize your photos with a third-party provider such as Flickr.

+ Post photos from Flickr to your blog with the **Blog this!** button.

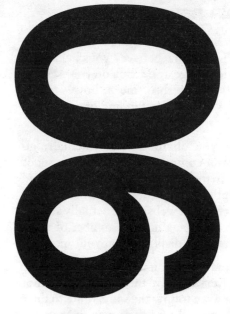

06

hosting your own blog

In this chapter you will learn:

- about domain names
- how to register your own domain name
- how to use your domain name for your blog

6.1 A bit of domain name theory

How does the Internet work? It's actually quite mind-boggling to try to comprehend all the work done between you clicking on a link in a webpage and the next page appearing on your screen. So we try not to, and suggest you do the same ... however, it is useful at this point to have a vague understanding of some of it, so bear with us.

When you 'visit' a website, you obviously don't actually go anywhere, and neither does your computer. Your computer sends a request for information out to the Internet; this request is passed around countless other computers in various places until it gets to a computer where the files for that website are actually stored. Then the information is sent back (again, via a number of other machines) to your computer, which displays it on your monitor.

During this process, the information is split up into small 'packets' of data to be transmitted. Remarkably, these packets do not necessarily travel together, or even follow the same route to their destinations – but somehow they all find their way to the right place and form themselves back into a coherent whole. How do they know where they're going? Well actually, the full details of that are far too full to go into here! But part of the answer lies in the domain name system (DNS).

IP addresses

Every computer connected to the Internet has an identification code called an *IP address* (IP stands for Internet Protocol), which computers use to identify each other on the network. IP addresses are sets of numbers which look like this: 192.168.138.67 – four numbers between 0 and 255 joined together with dots. This gives around 4.2 billion combinations – not bad for a short set of numbers, but not very user-friendly for us. Even back in the days before the Internet was a mass phenomenon – before it was even called 'the Internet' and only a handful of shadowy geeks fluent in machine code used it – even then, the geeks realized that humans are better at remembering words and names than long strings of numbers.

So the domain name system was invented. The idea was that we would give computers nice user-friendly names, and then associate these names with IP addresses. Then we can say to our computer (let's call it Norman) 'Norman, I want the latest news from the computer called Hedwig – go get it!' Norman rolls his digital eyes at our inefficiency and consults his internal address book. There he finds that when we say 'Hedwig' we really mean '255.255.37.127', so he sends a request to that computer.

'Hi 255.255.37.127, it's 187.95.202.4 here. Hope you're well. Can you send me the latest news please?'

'Sure 187.95.202.4,' says Hedwig. 'Coming right up. Good to hear from you again, give my regards to the printer and peripherals.'

We don't actually give computers simple names like Norman and Hedwig – in this case, Hedwig might be called 'news.bbc.co.uk' for instance. But DNS is more than just a handy way of remembering names. As described so far, the system relies on Norman and Hedwig knowing each other's IP addresses – but as new computers are added to the network, maintaining an up-to-date address book on each of these millions of computers becomes impossible. To make it more manageable, the network is broken up into a hierarchical structure, and certain bodies called *domain registries* are tasked with maintaining publicly-available, up-to-date addresses for their sections – they are *authoritative* for their *domains*. For instance, Verisign Inc. is responsible for managing the .com and .net top-level domains, so they have to maintain information on any domain name ending in .com or .net. In the UK, the registry responsible for all .uk domains is a not-for-profit company called Nominet UK. Some of these bodies are commercial companies; others are run by or on behalf of national governments.

Domain names and DNS lookups

Domain names consist of multiple parts called *labels*, separated by dots. The Top Level Domain (TLD) is the furthest-right label (e.g. .com, .gov, .uk, etc.). An authoritative DNS server doesn't need to know the *complete* address of every computer beneath it in the structure, only as far as the next level down. At that point, another DNS server will be responsible for resolving the next part of the name, and so on, until the name is narrowed down to a specific IP address. This repetitive process is called *recursing* or more informally as a *DNS lookup*.

For instance, suppose we want to read the news from the website news.bbc.co.uk. Before we even request the news itself from the BBC's news servers, we first need to do a DNS lookup to find out where to send the request. Our computer asks its DNS server (usually at your Internet service provider) to look up the IP address for this domain name. The request is first passed to the authoritative DNS server for all .uk domains, at Nominet UK.

Nominet's DNS server says 'Sorry, I don't know that IP address, but I do know a computer which can give you information about any .co.uk name – here's that computer's IP address.' So your request is then repeated to this computer (as it happens, Nominet manage this domain too, but in theory another registry could).

Anyway, it replies 'Nope, I don't know either – but I do know a computer which can tell you about all the .bbc.co.uk names – here's the IP address.' You're getting close, but you're not there yet! Your request is repeated to this third computer, which is somewhere in a BBC building. This one says 'news.bbc.co.uk? Yes, sure, I know that one – here's the IP address'.

Domain caching

In fact, a full recursive lookup does not happen every time you visit a website: your ISP will have a DNS server which *caches* or remembers the IP addresses for domain names which it's looked up before. Each domain name in this cache has an expiry date, set by the authoritative DNS server for that name. As long as the record is within its expiry date, the cached IP address is used; when it expires, a new lookup is performed.

6.2 Registering a new domain name

The domain name system is overseen by an international body called ICANN – the Internet Corporation for Assigned Names and Numbers. ICANN authorizes registries to administer the top-level domains, who in turn authorize other registries to administer domains at the next level. In fact, only these registries actually 'own' a domain in the legal sense. When you buy a domain name, you don't own it outright, but are actually leasing it for a period of time from a registry, though there are laws to protect you (the registrant) and your ownership of the leasehold.

WHOIS who?

Anyone can find out who the registrant of a domain name is by looking it up through the DNS system. These are called WHOIS lookups; as in 'Who Is the registrant of this domain?' You can run a WHOIS lookup from the relevant registry's website, or there are centralized services which search multiple registries for you. Try www.dnsstuff.com for instance, and type a domain name into the WHOIS lookup box – you can see the results on the next page.

You can theoretically register a new domain name directly with a registry yourself, but it is not recommended for non-expert users because you usually need to know how to configure DNS records properly! More often the transaction is carried out through a third party domain name registrar or reseller, who deals with the registry on your behalf and charges a small fee for its trouble.

Your ISP may well offer domain registration services, but it's worth shopping around. Prices are rarely very high, but they can still vary quite a lot from one registrar to another, and so can the package you actually get for your money. When comparing prices and services, here are a few points to bear in mind:

- How long is the registration valid for? Sometimes it's for just one year, sometimes you can buy two or three years at once.

- What will they give you in terms of setting up and handling email to this domain name?

- What control are you given over technical aspects such as DNS records for the domain? If you want to use this domain with a TypePad blog, you will need to ensure that they support *custom CNAME records*. These are the parts of the DNS

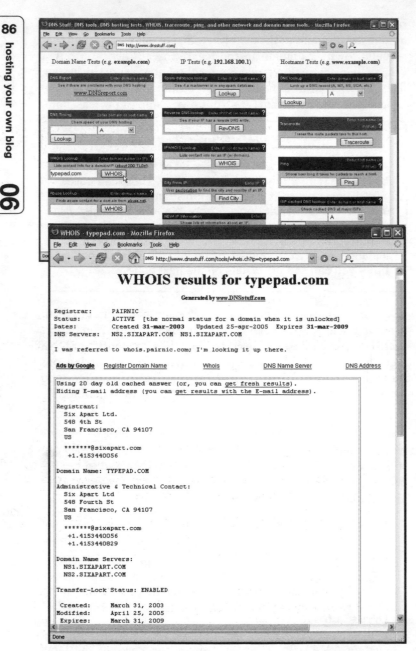

Running a WHOIS query from DNS stuff

record which you use to 'point' a domain at some other webspace – more on this later in this chapter.

- What else do you get? Does the package include webspace? How much? Do you get access to any site-building tools or other benefits?

- How much technical help will you get? If you want to create a separate sub-domain for each of your blogs, perhaps personal.myblog.com for your chronicles of toenail clipping, and political.myblog.com for where you set the world to rights. Will they do this for you? Do you need to edit the DNS records yourself? Will they help you at all?

- Are there any other ongoing or potential future charges, e.g. for technical help?

Choosing a domain name

You can choose any domain name you like, subject to a few restrictions. First, it must only consist of letters, the numbers 0–9 and the underscore character, with no spaces or other punctuation. Note that upper and lower case letters are treated the same – as some people have found to their cost. A famous example is the family counselling association in California which decided to set up a website to help people find suitable therapists near them, called TherapistFinder – so they registered therapistfinder.com, which can be read rather differently. The moral of the story: be careful with how your domain name will look when written all in lower-case letters! If it looks bad, consider an alternative or add an underscore: findatherapist.com or therapist_finder.com would be less ambiguous.

Second, it cannot be more than 63 characters long – but since half the point of having a domain name instead of an IP address is for it to be memorable to humans, that's probably a good thing!

And finally, you can't register a domain which someone else already has (obviously). But nor can you register a domain which would mislead people into thinking you represented some existing body. For instance, even if cocacola.com wasn't already registered, you couldn't register it unless you were genuinely doing so on behalf of the Coca-Cola corporation. This is called *cybersquatting* and it is subject to various forms of dispute resolution and legal protection in different countries.

Domain hacks

If you have a good head for lateral thinking, you might consider a *domain hack* instead of a straightforward domain name. Despite the term used, there's nothing underground or illegal about a domain hack. It's called a 'hack' in the sense of making a computer system do something it wasn't really intended to – not in the sense of hacking into computers. A domain hack is where you use the Top Level Domain label – usually a country code such as .us or .de – to make up part of a memorable word or name.

For instance, the blog-monitoring website blo.gs bought the domain label 'blo' under the '.gs' TLD (.gs is the country code for South Georgia and the South Sandwich Islands, a small UK overseas territory in the southern Atlantic). Or if Nat wanted a personalized website, he could register the domain name n.at using the Austrian country code TLD.

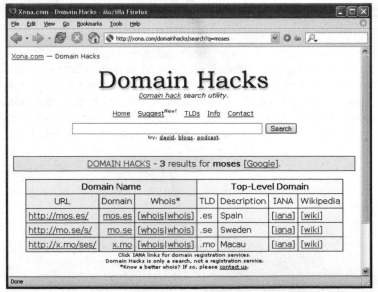

Why be restricted to a .com or .co.uk name?!

Domain hacks made easy

A neat little tool for finding domain hacks is available at
http://xona.com/domainhacks – type in the word you want
to make, and it will suggest suitable hacks.

6.3 Using your domain name

Now you have a nifty new domain name, how do you tie this in
to your blog? There are two methods: either your blog is actually
hosted on your own webspace, or it remains where it is and you
employ a technique called *domain mapping* to make it look as
though that's what's happening. The choice you make may be
made for you by the options offered by your blog provider: search
their Help section for information on using your own domain
name. We'll look at two examples: hosting a Blogger blog on
your own space, and mapping a TypePad blog to a domain.

Using Blogger and your own webspace

When you sign up for a Blogger account, you get 300Mb of
space for your pictures and an unlimited amount of space for
your posts – so you probably won't run out of space. But you
may have other reasons for wanting to host your blog on your
own space – it gives you a little more control and ownership of
it, or maybe you already have a website and the blog is just an
add-on to it. Whatever the reason, if you're doing it this way,
you probably don't need us to tell you how – which is just as
well, because we don't have the space to go into it in detail here
anyway! If you're *thinking* about hosting your own but aren't
sure, here's a brief outline of how the process works: after reading
this you should have a better idea of whether you want to try it
or not.

The first thing to do is to get yourself some webspace. As with
domain hosting, there are a million and one hosting services out
there offering a wide variety of packages, so do your homework.
Compare not just prices, but the amount of space you get with
each; how many email boxes; what email and website

management tools are provided; what technical support; what additional features and support for scripting or database hosting ... And don't get seduced by more features than you need – you don't need a secure server and 10 SQL databases if you're just hosting a blog! Check up on their record: find out what their uptime is – the percentage of time which their servers are working and fully available to the Internet. If it's less than 99.5% you're probably not looking at the most professional of hosts. Most importantly, get a recommendation from people who have their sites hosted there now – preferably people you know and trust!

When you buy your hosting space, you will be sent some account management information, including your FTP details. FTP (File Transfer Protocol) is the way data is handled when files are sent from one machine directly to another. Your hosting provider will give you an FTP account, which is a username and password with permissions to access certain parts of their web servers – your webspace – to upload and download files. If you're building your own website, you use FTP to upload web pages, images and other files from your computer to your webspace, usually via a desktop program called an FTP client.

FTP clients

You can find freeware and shareware FTP clients, or trial versions of full-featured paid-for clients, on the Internet. Commonly-used clients include WS FTP (www.ipswitch.com) and FileZilla (http://sourceforge.net/projects/filezilla) if you are working on a PC, and Fetch (http://fetchsoftworks.com) if you are a Mac user.

If you're using Blogger to do the technical work, all you need to do is to configure your blog to use those FTP details to publish your blog directly to your own webspace.

1 Log into your account, go to the **Settings** tab and click on **Publishing**. Near the top of the page, click on the link which says **Switch to: FTP**.

2 On the next page you will be prompted for information about your FTP account and webspace.

Blogger: It's Stupid, the Economy :: Publishing Settings - Mozilla Firefox

File Edit View Go Bookmarks Tools Help

http://www.blogger.com/blog-publishing.g?blogID=11668784   Go

It's Stupid, the Economy

← Back to Dashboard ? Help ✗ Sign Out

Posting **Settings** Template View Blog

Basic **Publishing** Formatting Comments Archiving Site Feed Email Members

You're publishing on blogspot.com

Switch to: FTP (publishing on your ISP server) Or SFTP (secure publishing on your ISP server)

Change your preference to FTP

Blog*Spot Address   http:// thestupideconom .blogspot.com

Subject to availability.

Notify Weblogs.com   No ▾

Weblogs.com is a blog update notification service that many individuals and services use to track blog changes.

Blogger: It's Stupid, the Economy :: Publishing Settings - Mozilla Firefox

File Edit View Go Bookmarks Tools Help

http://www.blogger.com/blog-publishing.g?blogID=116687848publish   Go

Posting **Settings** Template View Blog

Basic **Publishing** Formatting Comments Archiving Site Feed Email Members

You're publishing via FTP

Switch to: SFTP (secure publishing on your ISP server) Or blogspot.com (Blogger's free hosting service)

FTP Server   ftp.mydomain.com   ❓

Example: yourwebsite.com

Blog URL   http://www.mydomain.com/blog/

The web address where this blog is viewable. This should include http://.

FTP Path: /www/home/mydomain.com/blog/   ❓

This path must already exist on your server.

Blog Filename: index.html

Example: index.html

Warning: If this file already exists on your server in the path entered above, it will be OVERWRITTEN. Be sure to back it up.

FTP Username   myusername

FTP Password   ●●●●●●●●●●

Username & Password are optional. If you leave them blank, you will be asked to enter them when you publish your blog.

Notify Weblogs.com   No ▾

Weblogs.com is a blog update notification service that many individuals and services use to track blog changes.

Save Settings

http://help.blogger.com/bin/answer.py?answer=94

- **FTP Server –** this is the name of the computer to which your webspace is uploaded, and should be included in your FTP account information.

- **Blog URL –** this is the web address where people will go to view your site.

  If you have your own domain and will use it exclusively for your blog, then type in the domain name here, including the 'http://www.' at the start.

  If you have other content on this webspace, you probably want to put the blog files into a new folder and give the URL of this folder here.

- **FTP Path: –** this should also be supplied with your account information: it is the location of the folders where your web files are stored on your hosting provider's server. The path should correspond to the Blog URL you gave above.

- **Blog Filename: –** the filename of the front page of your blog: if you do not have any other content on your webspace apart from the blog, use *index.html* here. If *index.html* already exists and you want your blog to sit somewhere else, give it another name, such as *blog.html*.

- **FTP Username** and **Password –** your FTP account details. If you are a security-conscious type, you can leave these blank if you prefer, and enter them each time you publish a new post.

- **Notify Weblogs.com –** Weblogs.com is a blog tracking service which notifies subscribers when listed blogs are updated. If you turn this option on, then every time you post, it will be able to pass on the news to its subscribers.

3 Once you have entered the required information and saved it, you will need to republish your blog to transfer the existing posts to your webspace via FTP.

4 You should see a reminder of this after saving your changes – otherwise you can go to the **Posting** tab, click on **Status** and then hit the **Republish entire blog** button.

Browser window showing Blogger publish status page with "No publish results to display." and buttons "Republish Index Only" and "Republish Entire Blog".

Mapping your own domain to a TypePad blog

This is really not as hard as it sounds, but if monkeying about with technical settings makes you nervous, now is the time to stiffen your sinews, take a deep breath, reach for the whisky bottle in your desk drawer. No, just kidding – relax, it'll all be fine! TypePad does all the research and makes the decisions for you – all you have to do is carry out the instructions. Or you can just put in a request to your domain registrar to change the DNS settings for you (remember what we said earlier about checking out their technical help?).

Before you start, make sure you have everything to hand. When you registered your domain, you were probably sent some account details, which may include a username and password to log in and administer your account. Dig this out if you can find it – if not, contact your registrar and tell them you want to configure your DNS record. If you are going to try changing the settings yourself, ask them for your login details and instructions for accessing and editing the DNS settings. Most registrars have their own interfaces for editing DNS settings, so they'll all be slightly different. If you're going to get your registrar to edit the settings for you, make sure you have the right contact details, or you know how to submit a support request via their website.

1 Now log in to your account and go to the **Control Panel** tab.

2 Click on **Site Access** and then click the **Domain Mapping** submenu link. You'll see a notice reminding you that (a) you need a domain of your own before you can map it, and (b) to be careful when doing this, to avoid messing up your website or email! Don't panic, we know what we're doing.

3 Click the **Begin Here: Map a Domain Name** button to continue.

4 Type your domain name (without the 'http://www' bit at the start) into the box on the pop-up window. TypePad will query the current DNS record for your domain and display the settings you need to make the domain mapping work. Leave this window open, as you will need it and the details in it shortly. If you're asking your registrar to change the settings, send the details to them now and ask them to make the change.

If you're doing it yourself, here comes the tricky bit!

5 Log into your domain administration account and find the bit where you can edit DNS records. It'll be under 'DNS' or 'Domain Settings' or some such. Check the A and MX records against the details given by TypePad in the previous step.

https://www.typepad.com - TypePad - Mozilla Firefox

TypePad

Map a Domain: Updating your DNS Settings

1 Get DNS Settings

The first step in mapping a domain to your TypePad site is to configure the DNS record for your domain. To do this, your domain will need to be registered with a registrar that supports direct management of your DNS. Many registrars call this feature Custom DNS.

Enter your already-registered domain name below, then click the Get DNS Settings button. We will tell you the recommended settings for setting up Custom DNS at your registrar.

Enter your domain name: `itint.co.uk`   [Get DNS settings]

example.com
example.co.uk
subdomain.example.com

2 Configure Recommended DNS Settings

The next step is to enter the recommended DNS settings below in the management area of your domain registrar. We've provided shortcuts to some common registrars below (you will have to log in at their site if you haven't already).

A RECORD	MX RECORDS	CNAME RECORD
Domain: **itint.co.uk**	Domain: **itint.co.uk**	Domain: **itint.co.uk**
Address: **80.175.48.133**	Address: **adslmail1.ukisp.com**	Points to: **natty.typepad.com**
	Priority: **10**	

Here is a list of several popular registrars you may have registered with: (they will open in a new window)

Done   www.typepad.com

They should already be there – if they are not, or they are different from those which TypePad recommends, stop now and talk to your domain registrar before continuing. Assuming all is still OK, look for the bit where you can add a CNAME record. Enter your domain name and the address given by TypePad – something like *yourname.typepad.com* – then save or submit the record. Now before you do anything else, check what changes have been made!

Check your records carefully!

Once you've edited a DNS record, check it to make sure it all looks right. The interface for editing DNS records varies from one hosting provider to another, and some are not always very clear. On one, the field which looked like it should have the whole domain – 'www.itint.co.uk' – should actually only have had the 'www' subdomain. When we checked over the record, we saw that the CNAME record added was for 'www.itint.co.uk.itint.co.uk'! If this happens, don't panic – you can always edit or delete the record and start again.

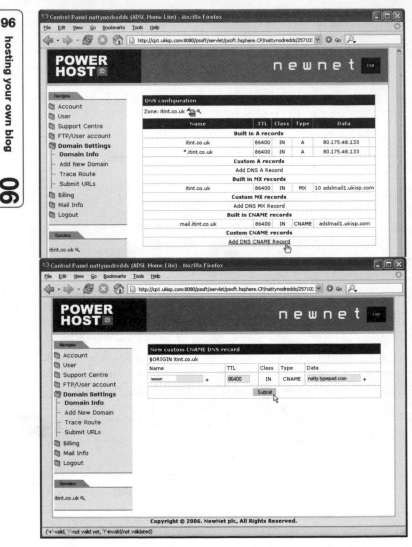

6 Your domain name is now configured to point to your TypePad blog, which means that when you type the domain name into a web browser, the blog should be displayed. It can however take a day or two for the new DNS information to propagate through the Internet, so some users, possibly including you, won't see the change immediately.

7 While you're waiting for that process to take place, there are a couple of configuration tasks to complete back at TypePad. You need to tell TypePad which blog or photo album is mapped to this new domain name, so it can create links to your posts with the correct address. Scroll down on the pop-up window which you left open a couple of steps back, and hit the **Complete Final Step** button.

8 On the next screen, select the blog or photo album that you want this domain to be mapped to, click **Add Domain** then click **Close Window** on the next page.

9 For the final step you'll need to wait until the DNS change has finished propagating: this might only take a couple of hours but you're better off calling it a day for now and coming back tomorrow. The next day, check that the DNS change has propagated by typing your domain name into a web browser: if you can see your TypePad blog, we're ready to go. If not, try again later. Once it's showing up as expected, log back into your blog and go to the **Control Panel** again. Click **Site Access** and then **Domain Mapping** – this time you should see your domain name listed in the bottom section, with a checkbox next to it labelled **Active**. Tick this box and click the **Set** button to finalize the mapping process.

Changing your DNS settings could adversely impact your email or other services that you rely upon. If it is done incorrectly. If you are unsure what you're doing, contact your registrar and ask them for support.

    Begin Here: Map a Domain Name

Your Domains

Below is the list of domains that you have already mapped to your TypePad site. To delete a domain mapping, check the Remove box in the table below, and press the Remove button. To activate a domain, check the Active box in the table below, and press the Set button.

Note: Do not set your domain as "Active" until you are sure that the domain's DNS record has been updated.

You have 1 domain in your list of mapped domains.

Domain	Mapped To	Active	Remove
itint.co.uk	natty.typepad.com/paradigmshift	☑	☐
		Set	Remove

TypePad © 2003-2006 Six Apart, Ltd. All Rights Reserved. | Terms of Service | Privacy Policy

Summary

+ The Domain Name System (DNS) is a way of organizing
  and finding data on the Internet.

+ Domain names map computer addresses to easy-to-
  remember words and phrases.

+ Register a domain name to give your blog its own web
  address.

+ Buy some hosting space for additional ownership of and
  control over your blog's files.

+ Connect your blog to your domain name and/or hosting
  space by domain mapping or hosting your own files.

+ Hosting your own files: set up your blogging service to
  transfer files directly to your webspace instead.

+ File Transfer Protocol (FTP) is how files are transferred
  from one computer directly to another.

+ Domain mapping: link your domain to your blog and then
  configure your blog to work with this domain.

07 advanced techniques

In this chapter you will learn:

- about **HTML** code for images and multimedia

- how to edit page templates

- how to blog by email and mobile phone

- about audio and video blogging

7.1 Web coding for bloggers

When you view a page on the Internet in your web browser, what happens? How does the browser know what colour to make the text, and where to put the picture of your mother-in-law in her party hat? The answer is code – web code. All web pages have to be marked up in the Internet's coding language, HTML (HyperText Markup Language for those of you with a penchant for acronyms), to give them a structure which can be understood by a web browser. These days, most webpages also use CSS (Cascading Style Sheets) for more flexible control over their visual appearance.

But so what? The whole point of blogging services is that they make web publishing accessible to anyone; you should be able to blog away merrily without having to learn any weird computer languages. And so you can, as long as your demands on the medium are not too onerous. As you type, format and add pictures, your blogging service beavers away behind the scenes, writing your code for you. But you may find after a while that you want to start pushing the boundaries of what the standard posting tools can offer you, and at this point you will need to start tinkering with the code behind the posts.

Brief introduction to HTML

We're not going to try to learn HTML properly now, because that's a book in its own right (yep, there's one in the *Teach Yourself* series!). But it's useful to understand some fundamentals before we move on to specific examples of code in action. The way code is used – which commands go where, how they're written and what information you need to attach to each one – is called syntax. The basic syntax of HTML involves taking a chunk of text that you want to do something to (italicize, for instance, or change the font), and wrapping it in little mark-up commands called tags. Look at the following example, where we take the word 'really' and make it bold by wrapping it in the tags for 'bold':

HTML is really pretty easy.

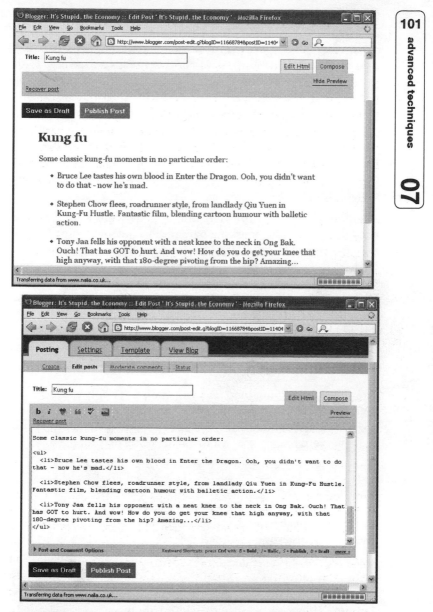

A blog page and the HTML code that produced it. The HTML tags used here produce a bulleted list: <ul>...</ul> (unordered list, tags go round the whole list) and <li>...</li> (list item, round each bullet point)

Tags are distinguished from the rest of the page text by being enclosed in <angle brackets>. The tags at the beginning and end of the chunk of text are identical, except that the closing one has a forward slash in it. When a web browser reads a page of HTML code, it displays anything *not* in angle brackets as text on the screen, so in the example above, 'HTML is' just comes out as plain text. When the browser gets to a bit of code inside <angle brackets>, it starts to apply whatever command is there; in the example this is 'make bold' – <b> – and so it displays the following bit of text in bold face. It then sees the 'stop making bold' tag – </b> – and returns to normal typeface for the remaining text 'pretty easy'.

There are other tags for changing typeface and size, text and background colours, marking paragraphs, indented 'blockquote' text, numbered and bulleted lists, creating hyperlinks, and more. Each of these has a start and end tag which is wrapped around the piece of text you want it to apply to, to get the desired effect. We won't go into details here, but if you flick between the compose and HTML modes of your blog's post editor, you'll quickly see how most of these work.

HTML for images

Then there are standalone tags which do not apply to a piece of text, but have their own purpose. For instance, <img...> does not have a start and end tag wrapped around some text, it's just a single tag which causes an image to be displayed:

<img src= "motherinlaw.jpg" />

In these cases, strict mark-up guidelines call for a closing slash before the end of the tag – you should try to keep to this to ensure your page is rendered properly, but generally you will get away with forgetting it sometimes!

Since tags of this sort do not apply to a piece of text, they need additional information to tell the browser what they *do* apply to. This information is given in bits called attributes – in the example above, we specify the src attribute as:

motherinlaw.jpg.

The <img... bit tells the browser 'put an image here', then the src=... bit tells it where to find the relevant file – the *source* of the image. Other attributes commonly used on an image tag can be added, to specify its size, border thickness, alignment to the surrounding text, and what should be shown if for any reason the image can't be displayed.

```
<img src="motherinlaw.jpg" width="200" height="150"
border="1" align="left" alt="Ha ha! Look at my mother in
law's funny hat!" />
```

The width, height, and border are defined in pixels. For reference, a standard blog template is about 750 pixels wide in total, but the width of the main posting column will depend on the template and layout you choose. With the alignment set to "left" or "right", the image is laid out to the left or right of any text *following* the image tag. The alt (*alternative text*) definition should be fairly brief and must **not** include double quotes – because a double quote will confuse the browser into thinking that this is the end of the attribute definition.

Web accessibility and images

Alt text is important for making your blog accessible to people with low or no vision. These users access the Internet using screen readers, which describe the page contents. Clearly no computer is clever enough to know that this picture is of your mother in law, or that you think her hat is funny. So to get the image across to someone who can't see it, *you* have to briefly describe it in words.

HTML for links

Although all blogging services will have a push-button approach to creating links, it is worth understanding how they work so that you can manage them more effectively, and troubleshoot when things go wrong! The tag used for creating links is the *anchor* tag, <a>...</a> with an href (*hyperlink reference*) attribute:

```
<a href="http://www.mysite.com">Link to my other site</a>
```

The first important thing to note is the http:// prefix to the URL of the page you are linking to. A common error when creating links to other pages is to miss this bit out and just jump straight into the www... bit. You *must* include it though, otherwise the browser will try to find a page called www.mysite.com somewhere on your current blog. But it doesn't exist there!

The next important thing is *where* this link is opened. Using this piece of code, the link will open up in the same window which your blog post was being displayed in. This is often fine, especially if the link is just to another page on your own blog. But you might be worried that your reader then follows a link on *that* page to another website, and then again to another site ... Then they might not be able to find their way back to your blog so they can finish reading your post!

To avoid this you can set another attribute which tells the browser to open a new window for the link – then when your visitor has finished exploring there, they can just shut that window down and your original post will still be visible in the window beneath. This is the target attribute, and you want to set it to _blank:

```
<a href="http://www.mysite.com" target= "_blank">Link</a>
```

Web accessibility and links

Again, this is an area where you should be considering accessibility issues. Switching between windows without warning can be confusing for people using screen readers, so you need to make it clear that this is going to happen *before* the user clicks on a link. You can do this using the title attribute:

```
<a href="http://www.mysite.com" target="_blank" title="This link opens www.mysite.com in a new window">Link</a>
```

CSS for style and layout

Using CSS style attributes in your HTML tags gives you much finer control over the visual appearance of the page. When HTML was originally developed, the Internet was a much simpler place.

People had slower connections and smaller, low-resolution monitors, so images were used less and no unnecessary bandwidth was given over to fripperies such as style and design ... a web page with a bit of flashing text was like, way out there, man. Since then of course, the world has moved on and we expect a much richer experience. HTML is still needed to give the page its structure, but we need more stylistic control as well. CSS was developed to fill this gap: it takes HTML elements – the building blocks of the page as defined by tags – and extends their visual properties so that you can do more with them.

For instance, rather than just defining the thickness of the border around an image using the border attribute, you can use CSS to set the thickness, colour and style of each side separately. So you could have a thick, red, solid border along the bottom but a thin, blue, dashed border along the top.

CSS styles are assigned to elements by including them in the relevant HTML tag under the style attribute. This attribute can hold many different style settings, called *properties*: in the example below, we set the width and alignment of an image, and the space left blank between it and any surrounding text or images.

```
<img src= "mypic.jpg" style="width:250px; float:left;
margin:5px;" />
```

This will left-align the photo, with text starting just to the right of it and then wrapping beneath the picture. Note that each style property is defined after a colon, and properties are separated by semi-colons. As with normal HTML attributes, the whole style definition is enclosed in double quotes.

So far, this is nothing which you couldn't already do in HTML, but if you try adding this code to a post, you'll see that it could be better. At the moment, the image is not flush with the edge of the text above and beneath it, because of that 5 pixel margin around it. Ideally, we want *no* margin above or to the left of the image, and let's say a 10 pixel margin beneath it and 5 pixels to the right.

We can do this in two ways. Either we set each margin individually:

```
<img src="mypic.jpg" style="margin-left:0px; margin-top:0px;
margin-bottom:10px; margin-right:5px;" />
```

Or we can use a shorthand method, in which all four margins are defined in turn, starting from the top and working clockwise:

```
<img src="mypic.jpg" style="margin: 0px 5px 10px 0px;" />
```

An <img... > tag using a linked image, with margins set by the CSS style property.

If you want a border round your images, you can include the border property in your image tag's style definition. This uses the syntax:

border: *width line-type colour*

The width is usually set in pixels. There are numerous line-types, including solid, dotted, dashed, double, or ridge. Some common colours such as red, blue, black, white, or yellow can be given in words; otherwise you will need the hexadecimal code for the colour (see opposite for more on this).

```
<img src="mypic.jpg" style="border: 2px solid black;" />
```

A note on hex colours

Colour settings on webpages are given as *hexadecimal* values – numbers in mathematical base 16. Normally when we count we use base 10, *aka* the decimal system, basically because we have ten fingers. You can count up to ten on your fingers, and we can call ten a 'handful'. If you want to count eleven things, you have one handful ('1') and one unit ('1') which are written together as '11'. Twenty-six is two handfuls ('2') and six units ('6') which makes '26'.

Computers don't have fingers or hands, for them everything boils down to ones and zeroes in the end – this is a base 2 or binary system. Humans find binary very hard to work with, but hexadecimal offers a good compromise. It is a multiple of 2 ($2 \times 2 \times 2 \times 2$ or 2^4), and so can be converted to binary very easily, but it also produces numbers that humans can recognize and pronounce easily. When counting in base 16, when we get to 10 things, we haven't got a 'handful' yet, because that's 16 things – but we've run out of single-digit numbers to represent '10', so we start to use letters instead. Counting up to twenty in decimal and hex looks like this:

Dec	1	2	3	4	5	6	7	8	9	10	11	12	13	14	15	16	17	18	19	20
Hex	1	2	3	4	5	6	7	8	9	A	B	C	D	E	F	10	11	12	13	14

When we specify a hex colour for something on a web page, we use a six-digit code to set the *RGB values* – the balance between Red, Green and Blue. Each colour gets two hex digits – that's 0 to 255 in decimal – and ranges from 00 (no colour at all) to FF (very bright), and the combination of the three RGB settings gives you the overall colour. For instance:

000000 = black

FFFFFF = white

FF0000 = bright red

009900 = mid green

000033 = dark blue

So far, so good – but just to complicate matters further, the rules for combining colours in light are different from mixing paint. With paints, red and green make brown: with light, it makes yellow. Sorry, but your art class colour wheel won't help you here!

And as with the margin property, you can set borders differently for each edge of the picture – try this, for example:

```
<img src="mypic.jpg" style="border-top: 4px solid black;
border-right: 2px dotted blue; border-bottom: 8px groove
orange; border-left: 2px dotted green;" />
```

WARNING!

You may want to take advice from a qualified designer before ruining the visual appeal of your blog with wacky over-excited style settings! Use with moderation.

CSS for formatting text

CSS does not only work with images – you can apply styles to any HTML element, including chunks of text. Most blogging services give you some control over text styles and colours, but you can extend the range of options substantially with CSS.

A common way of styling some text is to enclose it in ... tags, for instance:

```
I cannot <span style="color: red; font-size: 200%; font-
weight: bold;">stress</span> this point <span style="font-
style: italic; font-family: arial; text-decoration:
underline;">enough</span>!
```

Some key properties to bear in mind for text formatting:

- **font-family** – the name of the typeface. Best to use only standard fonts – if your readers don't have your favourite crazy font installed on their machines, they will see a plain substitution instead.

- **font-weight** – normal, bold or extra-bold.

- **font-size** – this can be defined in pixels, but it is bad practice to do so, as you will make it difficult for readers with low vision to read your blog. The best option is to work with *relative sizes* – e.g. font-size:50% makes this bit of text half as big as the surrounding text.

- **text-decoration** – underline, overline, line-through or none.
- **color** – sets the text colour in *hexadecimal* RGB values (see page 107).

Text formatted using styles defined in a <span ...

Putting CSS and HTML together

We've seen above how to define CSS properties inside HTML tags to apply style settings to that particular page element. This is fine for making occasional *ad hoc* adjustments to formatting, but if you want to apply a certain style to many similar page elements, there is a more efficient way of doing it. You can define a suite of style settings called a *class*, which is applied to all matching elements.

The class is defined near the beginning of the page code, in the <head> section, and it needs to be placed between <style> ... </style> tags. Then, depending on the way we define the class, it is either applied to *all* page elements marked with a matching HTML tag, or only to those which we mark up with a class attribute.

In the example below we first create a class to be applied by default to *all* images, by referencing the HTML <img.../> tag in the class name, and then defining style settings between {curly braces}. Then we create a second class which we only want to use for *some* images: this will be a sub-class of images where we want to align the image right instead of left. We do this by inventing a sub-class name which starts with a dot (full stop/ period symbol). When we want to apply this style to a particular image, we call up this new class by name.

Style code in the page <head>:

```
<style>
    img { float: left; margin: 0px 10px 10px 0px; }
    img.RightAlign { float: right; margin: 0px 0px 10px 10px; }
</style>
```

Using the classes in the page <body>:

```
<img src="pic1.jpg">This text will appear to the right of this
standard left-aligned image...
<p/>
<img src="pic2.jpg" class="RightAlign">...whereas this
image references our new sub-class defined for right-
aligning images.
```

You will probably need to make use of this system of defining and using classes when you edit your blog post templates. If you look at a standard piece of template code you will see a long list of class definitions, some of which are recognizable as standard HTML elements, while others are prefixed with dots, hashes and @ symbols. The table below helps to explain these:

Prefix	Description
[none]	Class name is a standard HTML tag code, e.g. h1, h2, img, p, body, etc. This defines a default style for all matching HTML elements.
.	Defines a sub-class. If there is an HTML tag name *before* the dot (e.g. img.RightAlign), then this sub-class can *only* be applied to images. If the class name just starts with the dot (e.g. .RightAlign), then you can apply this class to *any* tag – to right-align a chunk of text, for instance.

Prefix	*Description*
#	Defines a class which applies to just one specific page element. The chosen element is marked up with an id property. For instance, a class called #SideColumn will *only* be applied to an element which has the property id="SideColumn" defined, e.g. <div id="SideColumn">.
@	Used for advanced style set-up commands. For instance, in your blog templates you may find a set of classes defined within a class marked @media handheld. This adjusts the style settings to suit mobile devices with small screens. Unless you really know what you are doing, you should probably leave these settings alone, as they will be optimized already!

7.2 Editing page templates

All blogging services should allow you to edit your page templates to some degree, but the way this is handled varies substantially. Our two example services, Blogger and TypePad, approach the matter from opposite directions. Blogger gives you access to all the raw code and says 'Here you go pal, knock yourself out!' while TypePad offers a beginner-friendly interface for editing some basic features, but only gives full design control to users paying for a premium account.

When you do get your hands on the code, you will find yourself faced with HTML and CSS code, which by now should seem at least vaguely familiar. You will also find some proprietary code which varies from service to service: these give you control over which elements of your blog appear where – post headers, sidebar links, your profile picture, and so on.

But let's start with the basic TypePad template-editing interface and move on to more complex editing in a moment.

Editing templates in TypePad

To start tinkering with your template, log into your account and go to **Weblogs**.

1   Now click on the **Edit Design** shortcut link and then **Manage Your Designs**. You should now see a list headed **Your Saved Designs** (there'll only be one in there at the moment).

2   The first thing to do is to create a duplicate of the one you have at the moment, so if it all goes completely pear-shaped, you can abandon it without having messed up the current design. You can save as many designs as you like and switch between them until you settle on one you like.

3   Tick the box next to the template name and then hit the **Duplicate** button; a copy of that template now appears in the list. Notice that under the **Options** column, the original template is marked **Currently Applied Design** – this shows which template is currently active – while the new duplicate

design has two links: **Preview** and **Apply Design.** Use these links to check your designs and apply the one you want.

4 Now we'll start editing the template: click on the duplicate template name and select the **Theme** link from the mini-menu which appears. At the top, change the radio button selection from **Pre-defined Theme** to **Custom Theme.** TypePad breaks down the page into four modules, each of which can be edited to adjust the relevant colours, fonts and borders:

- **General Page Settings** – this sets the basics: background colours and borders; column widths; and the colours of hyperlinked text. Note that the options for specifying column widths here will depend on the arrangement of columns in the basic layout you have chosen.

- **Page Banner** – the banner runs across the top of your page, where the blog title sits: edit the banner colour and borders; font, font size and colours; or use an image instead of text for the title.

- **Weblog Posts** – this sets the style for the main content of your page, the posts. Edit border styles and fonts, sizes and colours for the four components of each post: title, date, body and footer.

- **Sidebar Items** – the sidebars are the slimmer columns where you typically feature your profile, favourite links, and so on. Edit the fonts, sizes and colours for item titles and content; set border styles for images; and colours for hyperlinks.

5 Start with the general page settings. Click the button to open the editing interface in a pop-up window.

This breaks down the page further into general colour and border settings, hyperlink colours, and then separate sections for each column. In each case there's a little diagram on the left showing you which part of the page you're dealing with, and a preview of the colours and border styles you've chosen.

On the right you have your tools for editing the settings for that section: drop-down menus for the column widths and border settings; clickable colour spectrums and free-text fields for the colour settings (see page 107 for an explanation of the colour codes).

6   Have a play around with these and check out the effects in the preview sections on the left, then click **Save Changes** to close the pop-up and return to the main template editing page.

7   Do the same for each of the other page modules: with these you will also have font styles and sizes to choose from as well as colours and borders.

8   When you've finished, hit **Preview** to see how the new settings will look when applied to your blog, then go back and tweak the settings as needed.

9   When you're happy with your work, click **Save Changes**, then go back to the **Manage Your Designs** screen.

10 Click the **Apply Design** link next to the relevant template name: this makes your new design the new active design, but does **not** immediately affect the existing pages on your blog. To make the changes actually carry through to your blog, you need to hit the **Republish Weblog** button.

Editing complex templates

Note that the basic template editor only works with normal ('classic') layouts, not TypePad's 'mixed media' layouts. If you've opted for one of these calendar-style templates and want to edit it, you will need to upgrade to a Pro membership and work with the advanced template editor. See page 116.

With the changes all in place, it's time to publish them

Template code in TypePad

To get your hands on the template code in TypePad you will need to be signed up for a Pro account. If you don't have this you can make some limited adjustments to style settings using the template editor (see page 112 above).

1 To upgrade your account to Pro, go to the **Control Panel** tab and click on **Account Info**, then on **Upgrade/Downgrade Account.** Select the **TypePad Pro** option and then hit the **Change My Membership** button.

2 Confirm your decision in the pop-up window and you are instantly upgraded.

3 If you're still reading now, we'll assume you've done this! Go to the **Design** section of your blog and click on **Manage Your Designs.** You should see a list of **Your Saved Designs:** tick the checkbox next to the one you want to use as the basis for your customization and then hit the **Convert to Advanced** button.

Upgrading a TypePad account

4 Confirm this in the pop-up window, then you'll see a new design added to your list: this one will have a little cog icon next to it to show that it's an *advanced template*, i.e. one you can edit the code for.

5 Click on the new template name and then click **Edit**. This lists a suite of templates needed for different parts of your site – the ones you'll be mostly interested in are the Main Index, Archive Index, Sidebar and Stylesheet.

6 Click on one to start working with that template.

TypePad's templates are made up of small modules which can be edited separately and reused in other templates. This is a neat and efficient way of coding pages, especially from a maintenance point of view: anything that might be used more than once can be changed in one place only, and the changes are instantly picked up wherever they're needed. Unfortunately it can make life a little awkward for the beginner trying to make sense of the templates, because you can't easily see the whole code together: you have to build up your understanding of the template piece by piece.

Template code in Blogger

Blogger's approach to template management is more cavalier than TypePad's, which you may find refreshing or slightly daunting, depending on your appetite for getting down and dirty with page code. Moreover, you can't store multiple design templates as in TypePad – so when you make changes to the template, you have to decide right there and then whether to keep the changes or scrap them. You don't have the luxury of being able to draw up a few designs and then spend a few days coming back to them with a fresh eye now and then before making a decision. But hey – this is a free service, so you can't have everything! Just be warned, and tread carefully when implementing a redesign. If decisiveness isn't one of your strengths, you may want to take screenshots or print off the preview pages, and copy and paste the template code into a file on your computer. Then you *can* try out a few designs and take your time over the decision – it's just not as convenient.

Assuming that hasn't put you off (be brave!) and you're ready to have a go, log into your Blogger account, open your blog and go to the **Template** tab. The main item on this page is a text window containing a lot of scary-looking code. We'll come back to this in a moment: the other item is a drop-down menu to select the colour of the **Blogger NavBar**. This is the strip along the top of your blog containing the Blogger logo, search box and links to other parts of the Blogger site. The navbar is a non-negotiable part of your blog; it's the price you pay for having free webspace. You do however have a limited number of colour schemes to choose from so that it blends in with your blog reasonably closely.

The scary-looking code

So – now to the scary-looking code! Depending on your blogging service, this may be all given in one big file, or it may be split into sections. Sometimes CSS style definitions are put into a separate file called a *stylesheet* which can then be applied to

Plan B: 'Run away! Run away!'

With some services such as TypePad you can store and switch between multiple templates, so there's little danger of making unfixable mistakes. Even if you do have this safety net, it's still worth making a backup Plan B before you jump in and start editing. Copy the entire contents of the code window, paste them into a text file and save them somewhere. Now if you mess things up, you can copy this backup-template code into the window: no lasting damage done and less time wasted trying to find out where you messed up! You may also find it easier to work with the code in a text editor rather than in the small template-editing window, so you've got more room to see what's going on.

more than one template. However it is made available to you, the code falls into three categories: CSS style settings, HTML and proprietary code. You may want to refer back to the table on page 111 above to help you understand how the styles are used. The proprietary code belongs to your blogging service and will vary from one service to the next. It will consist of code to tell the blogging engine where to put things, e.g.

```
<$BlogPostTitle$>
```

or

```
<$MTInclude module="banner"$>
```

There will also be XHTML (eXtended HTML) tags such as <BlogDateHeader> or <PostBody> which logically mark out the page elements. These tags are important for syndicating content via feeds (see Chapter 9).

If the templates have been coded sensibly you should see some *code comments* which will help you make sense of the template. These do not affect the way the page is displayed, they are just there to act as signposts for humans looking at the code. For instance, you might see a line like this:

```
<!— Main Column —>
```

This indicates where the code setting out the main column of the template begins. HTML comments begin with <!— and end with —> (possibly several lines later). The style section may also have

Code for the main column starts here

Body content of the post goes here

comments, which are prefixed by a double slash or enclosed in slashes and asterisks:

```
/* general page elements */
// link style
a { text-decoration: underline; }
```

Have a look through the template file(s) and try to identify roughly where the major page elements are – where the page header is, where the main body content of your post goes, where the sidebar code is (assuming you have a layout with a sidebar!). Ignore all the detail for now, just try to work out the broad structure of the page. Then look at each bit in turn and dissect it a bit further. If there aren't any comments in the code, look for tags with descriptive names like <ArchiveTitle> and try to match them up with elements you know exist on the page.

Editing TypePad modules

TypePad takes a very modular approach to its templates. When you edit a TypePad template, you actually won't see much HTML or style code, because most of it is set in the modules themselves. You can create your own modules and pull them into a template using the code, but this is quite difficult to do from scratch – you want an existing module to work from. Rather unhelpfully, there does not appear to be an easy way to access these from the template editing screen, and you need to go to the Help section and search for *default template modules* to find them. Copy the code, then return to the editing screen and click 'Create new template module', then paste the code into the window, edit it and save with a suitable name. You can pull this new module into a template using the code <$MTInclude module="module_name"$>.

Which bits do I edit?

You will generally not need to mess with the proprietary code much. You should be able to use your blogging service's own interface for adding, removing and re-ordering components of the template, such as having archive links in the sidebar. Where this is possible, it's best to do it via the interface because (a) it's easier and (b) you're less likely to introduce bugs. However, you should still familiarize yourself with the tags because it will help you get a feel for what's on the page and how it fits together.

There will probably also be some optional proprietary tags which do not feature in the standard templates but which you can use if you like. For instance, in Blogger you can insert information from your profile page using tags such as:

    <$BlogOwnerAboutMe$>

and

    <$BlogOwnerLocation$>

The names of these tags and how they can be used will vary substantially from one blogging service to the next, so we won't try to cover them all here. Look in the Help section of your chosen service for 'template tags' or 'customizing templates' to see what they have to offer.

Most of the changes you will make will actually be to the CSS; you just need to understand the XHTML and proprietary tags so you can work out which bits of the CSS definitions to work on. Sometimes you'll need to look quite carefully to find this! For instance, the example below is a code snippet from the front page of a blog, which displays the post title, linked to the post's own page. In amongst all the XHTML tags, you could easily miss the <h2> tags – but this is what you actually need to know!

```
<BlogItemTitle><h2><BlogItemURL><a
href="<$BlogItemURL$>"></
BlogItemURL><$BlogItemTitle$><BlogItemURL></a></
BlogItemURL></h2></BlogItemTitle>
```

But how do you know which bits you need to know?! If you look through the style code at the top of the page, you won't find any classes defined for <BlogItemTitle> or <BlogItemURL>, so you know that these can't be how the heading style is defined. The hyperlink tag <a...> *does* feature in the style section, but it only gives limited style information. Besides, there are other links on the page which do not appear in the large title-sized font, so you know there must be something else involved. That just leaves the <h2> tag. To be sure, try a simple edit on the h2 class definition: change the colour and then preview the page. Check that the title has indeed changed colour – and also that nothing else has changed! The <h2> tag could be used for some other part of the template, in which case you could change more than you meant to. If this happens, create a sub-class h2.main and edit just that <h2> tag to add a class="main" attribute to it. Then there's no confusion.

7.3 Blogging on the road

Holiday checklist: sun cream, check; Tagalog phrasebook, check; clean underwear, check; blog ... blog! Don't forget the blog! Fortunately, bringing the blog doesn't mean trying to pack your 19" monitor into a suitcase. You can of course access your blog from any computer, not just your own, as long as you have your username and password with you. You can borrow a machine or sit down in an Internet café and blog away. But there are other options too: you can post to your blog via email and from your mobile phone.

Blogging by email

Why email? If you've got to sit at a computer anyway, why not log in and blog normally? Well, if you're somewhere with limited Internet access, it is useful to be able to compose an email offline and then just connect very briefly to send it. And sometimes it's simply more convenient, or how shall we say, *expedient*, to fire off an email instead of being logged into a blogging site. From the other side of the office, for instance, writing an email looks just like work!

Whatever your reasons for blogging by email, the first thing to do is to set up your blog to take incoming email posts. For your blog to be sure that it's really *you* sending it posts, it will want to establish some security procedures. These vary from service to service: it may ask you for a hard-to-guess address to send your posts to, or it might ask you for a confirmation address: then when it receives a post by email, it will send you a return message which you must reply to, before the post is published.

Setting up at Blogger

Blogger uses the first method, a secret email address.

1   To set up your Blogger account to receive email posts, go to the **Settings** section and click on **Email**.

2   Ignore the top box for now – unless you want Blogger to email you a copy of your posts when they're published (perhaps you want to keep a record of your work offline). Below that, you are prompted to enter a secret word which forms part of your unique **Mail-to-Blogger** email address. Choose something which you will remember – but which will be hard for anyone else to guess!

3   If you want emailed-in posts to be published immediately, tick the **Publish** checkbox, or leave it blank if you want them to be saved as drafts for later publication.

4 Click **Save Settings** and you are ready to go. Just put the post title in the subject line of your email, and the post itself in the body, then send to your Mail-to-Blogger address.

Keeping secrets secret

If your email blogging is via the hard-to-guess email address method, you need to be able to keep a secret! Don't store your secret email address anywhere where it might be accessible to others. If other people have access to your computer, delete any copies of the email from your Sent items and Trash boxes. If you are asked to supply part of the secret address, don't use anything obvious like 'password' or 'opensesame'. Try to avoid things which other people could easily work out, like your birthday or nickname – the safest thing is to make it as random as possible.

Setting up at TypePad

TypePad gives you a choice of security measures: a secret email address, a confirmation email or, more sophisticated, an encrypted key method. We'll look at each of these in a moment.

1 First, log in to your account and go to the **Profile** section, under **Control Panel**, then click **Mobile settings**.

2 If you have more than one blog or photo album, select the one you want to post to by default.

3 Add in any email addresses you want to be able to blog from. This is an extra level of security – even if someone *does* guess your secret email address, TypePad will only accept posts from the addresses listed here.

Security tip: don't print your secret email address in a book!

4 Now choose a security method: secret email address, confirmation before publishing, or PGP signatures.

We've already discussed the first two methods, which are simple but effective (if in doubt, go for the secret email address). The third is more sophisticated: PGP is an encryption standard, short for Pretty Good Privacy. This is actually an understatement – you might not want to post the firing code for an atomic weapon under PGP, but it is certainly as secure as you could ever want for a blog! To email posts using PGP, you will need to have a PGP-compliant email program with a key enabled. We can't really cover this in detail here – if you are keen to use PGP you can find out more about it at www.pgp.com.

5   To post to your default blog, just email to the secret address from one of your authorized email addresses, putting the post title in the subject line and the post in the message body.

If you have more than one blog and want to post to a different one, type the blog name *before* the post, separated by a colon. For instance, suppose you have two blogs called *Confessions Of A Furniture-Waxer* (set as the default) and *French Polishing For Industry Insiders*. If you email a post in with the subject line:

Mind your own beeswax

it will be published to *Confessions Of A Furniture-Waxer*. If you want to post it to the other blog, type in the subject line:

French Polishing For Industry Insiders: Mind your own beeswax.

This use of the colon may have set alarm bells ringing, and rightly so – if you try to email in any post with a colon in the title, TypePad will think you're trying to post it to a specific blog and will fail to post it properly. When posting by email, you will have to think of ways round this. If you want a post called *Wax: to bee or not to bee?* use a hyphen or ellipsis instead of a colon.

Moblogging

Mobile phone blogging, or 'moblogging' is really just sending emails from your phone. There are some services which allow you to send pictures and text via MMS (Multimedia Messaging Service) to your blog, but this star is likely to be eclipsed by email as the transmission protocol of choice. In either case, the procedure for moblogging is basically the same as for blogging by email. You set your blog up to receive posts by email, then compose your post – on your phone instead of on a computer – and send it to the appropriate email address. If you're using TypePad or another service which checks incoming posts against a list of authorized email addresses, you will need to find out what your phone's email address is.

Check with your mobile service provider

Not all mobile phones or service agreements will have what you need to moblog properly, or they may not have the necessary features enabled by default. You may need to ask your mobile network operator whether you can send emails from your phone, and if so, how you go about it.

Some mobile phone manufacturers and network operators offer specific blogging products and add-ons for your phone. Nokia, for instance, has a piece of software called **Lifeblog** which you can download and install on selected phones. It organizes any multimedia files it finds on your phone into a timeline, and can be integrated with a TypePad weblog for easy blogging of pictures, video and audio from your phone.

Video and audio blogging

There are two ways of putting sound and video clips into a post. The first is to embed the clip into the page so that it plays within the blog page itself. This can still be an area fraught with complexity, because there are many competing audio/video formats and media players. *Most* players can handle *most* formats, but it's still hard to be sure you're providing something which your whole audience can experience. One safe option is to convert the audio or video into a Flash format. The Adobe (formerly Macromedia) Flash Player is bundled into most new browsers, and they reckon they now have 98% coverage of Internet users.

You can create video files in this format using Flash Professional, but for most home users the price tag on this will put you off. Alternatively there are a number of cheap or shareware programs available online which will convert other video formats into Flash. Some of these will also generate the HTML code you need to embed the file into your page. Try searching for "flash video converter" – but as with all free or cheap downloads, satisfy yourself that the software you're getting is safe and legitimate before you install it on your computer or hand over credit card details!

The second and generally preferable option is to provide a link to the clip so that your readers can click on it *if* they want to, and they can watch or listen to it using *their* preferred media player. If you have a TypePad blog, you can do this very easily – just use the **Insert File** button to upload the file and create a download link to it automatically. If your blogging service does not offer a similar option, you will need some webspace to upload your file to, and make a note of the URL. That part's beyond the scope of this book, but once you've got it, you can use your blogging service's normal **Hyperlink** button to create the download link to it.

Third-party audio and video services

There are a growing number of third-party products which can be hooked into established blogging services to add video and audio to your blog. We can't cover these in detail in this book, but here are a few examples:

• **Blogger and Audioblogger** – sign up for a free account at audioblogger.com and configure it to link up with your Blogger blog. Then call a special number from any phone, anywhere, and an MP3 audio file will be recorded, saved, and a link added to your blog automatically – magic! Only available in the US at present, but there are plans to roll it out to other countries soon.

More details at http://audioblogger.com/faq.html

• **TypePad and VideoEgg** – sign up for a free account at VideoEgg and you can get an integrated VideoEgg / TypePad interface which allows you to convert your video files to Flash and embed them easily in your posts.

More details at http://typepad.videoegg.com/faq.html

- **TypePad and Vlog it!** – Vlog it! is a drag-and-drop desktop application used to edit video, still images and audio into an all-singing, all-dancing multimedia package, complete with whizzy scene transitions and sound effects. The basic version is free and the makers hope you'll be hooked enough to upgrade to the paid-for full version before long.

More details at http://www.sixapart.com/vlogit/

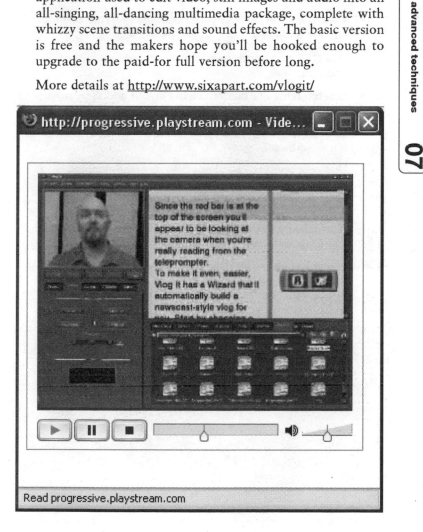

Summary

- Take more control over your posts using HTML code for images and links.

- Use CSS to extend your formatting options for images and text.

- Edit templates to customize the layout and appearance of your blog.

- Set up your blog to receive posts by email at a secret email address.

- Use your phone to send posts to an email-enabled blog.

- Add video and audio to your blog by embedding Flash files or linking to other formats.

- Alternatively, use a third-party add-on product to do your video/audio blogging.

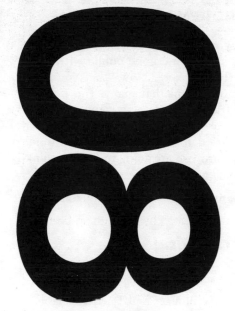

08
reaching your audience

In this chapter you will learn:

- how to promote your site
- about search engines
- about networking

8.1   How to promote your site

You're up and running with your weblog, you've overcome your shyness; you've tested your system and gone public with your unique contribution to the blogosphere. Now what you need are some visitors. You may not want that many, you may be happy with just family and friends or you may want to try and become one of the superstar elite of webloggers whose sites attract the kind of attention that used to be reserved for national newspapers. Whatever your aims you are going to have to think about marketing and publicizing your site in some way.

There are automatic and manual ways of promoting your site.

8.2 Automatic promotion

Ping

Most hosted weblog systems like Blogger and Typepad enable a simple program called **Packet Internet Groper** or **Ping**, which if activated for your weblog will automatically send a message to servers which aggregate all the latest weblog posts from around the world. Sites like Weblogs.com and Technorati use these automatic update notifications from sites like yours to build aggregated views of latest posts and other dynamic blog data. Simply by changing some settings on your hosted service, every time you post, the main aggregators are pinged and your site gets a little boost across the network.

If you don't have a hosted service or you're interested to get more out of the Ping system, you can register your site with free services like Pingomatic. Sites like this will watch your site for updates and then ping the most popular aggregators.

Trackback/Email this post

Each post in a weblog will have its own unique web address or URL (Universal Resource Locator). In blogging this is often referred to as a 'Trackback' and in many systems each post will carry a trackback link at their foot. This enables visitors to the

Technorati – www.technorati.com – based on Pings to Weblogs.com, Technorati is a site which brings together a summary of all the latest posts and lets users and other sites look at a dynamic slice of all that's hot online. Imagine your site listed here!

Pingomatic – www.pingomatic.com – More Ping power! A free service for those whose self-built or hosted blog systems don't support Ping and for those who just want more Ping than their hosts can provide

site to generate a URL for the post which they can then use as a reference to your site from theirs. If you like, it's a way of making a deep link to a part of one blog from another. Potentially this is of mutual benefit. Your site gets promoted to readers of theirs, and theirs gets in front of readers of yours. What's great about this, is that it happens at an in-depth level so your site is presented in an extremely relevant, topical way. We'll come back later in this chapter to the importance of relevance and niche on a topic.

Related to the notion of trackback and unique referencing for posts is the idea of enabling visitors to email a link for your posts. Often in hosted systems this feature can be switched on, or in a home-built system you might want to consider implementing it as it facilitates that holy grail of marketing, 'word-of-mouth' or what has become known in the modern era as 'viral marketing'. The reason that this is so powerful is self-evident. Think about your own situation – you tend to react much more favourably to recommendations of goods and services from friends and family as it is more likely that you trust them, they know you and your taste and interest so their tips have much more credibility. A marketing message from some faceless corporation or their agency flunkies is inevitably going to carry less weight with you, no matter how well told or how well they've identified your needs based on past purchases. So, a reader recommending you to a friend is many times more likely to get you a new reader than any other kind of promotion you could run. Therefore, be easy to recommend, give your advocates the tools to pass on the buzz!

Enable RSS

Another amazing innovation of weblogs is the system of Really Simple Syndication or RSS. We'll look at this in more detail in the next chapter, but here's a brief introduction.

RSS enables the creation of feeds to which other sites or software such as newsreaders can be subscribed. This means that your content can automatically be syndicated and consumed in places other than your site. Before you start worrying that someone is stealing your stuff remember that this distribution of your content is in the end going to increase your readership through promotion by wider distribution. In most systems you can set levels for how much of your material you want to show in RSS. Maybe just the title of the post and the first line, or the title and the tags or categories you've assigned to it. Whatever you do, just make sure you enable some kind of RSS on your site. Again, this way of releasing content from the instance of its publication on your site will pay off well in terms of increasing the reach of your site and the loyalty of your readers. And you don't have to make any effort, just set it up, switch it on and let your audience consume you in the most convenient way for them.

Reciprocal ads

There are systems of ad sharing such as Pheedo which you can integrate with your site. The concept of this is quite straightforward. Everyone in the system agrees to make space on their site and display ads which are then automatically included in their pages. These ads are simple, text-based boxes. In return, you create an ad for your site which is then displayed by the system on the partner sites, usually via some keyword matching of shared interest between your site and theirs.

Pheedo – www.pheedo.com – offers an example of collaborative advertising

Search engines

Simply put, if your blog is interesting, useful or helpful to others on the Web to the point where other sites will link to you, then you will achieve a higher ranking in search engines. Google, the most used search on the Web, works by looking at all the sites that link to you and analysing their importance as referees. Their relative importance is in turn measured on the sites that link to them and their importance. You can see that if you are lucky enough to get a link to your site from a very highly linked-to site, that is, one that is popular and highly regarded, this will be worth a lot to you in terms of search engine listing.

The great thing about blogs is that multiple links from lesser sites can still ramp up your score, as you gain a cumulative boost from all of their rankings. Search engines use automated programs called spiders, crawlers or bots to browse the Web, following links and recording information about the sites and pages that they find. In a way, you have to think about search engines as readers of your site, albeit robotic computer-controlled ones – so it makes sense to ensure your site is friendly to those programs and makes it easy for them to 'read' your links and pages.

If you can, make sure that the title of your blog carries the top keywords for your site. This may include your name or your company's and the main subject matter of your blog. This should also carry over into post titles. Try to reference the main subject of the post, even if you're doing this in a witty or elliptical way. If you'd like help with working out good keywords to use, you could try tools such as Overture's Keyword Suggestion Tool or WordTracker.com. You should also try to ensure that your posts have static HTML references (in weblogs known as a permalink) rather than dynamic links. The easiest way to spot a dynamic link is a question mark in the URL. If you can, you need to set up your blog to create permalinks instead of or as well as dynamic ones.

The final point on being accessible to search engines is to make sure that as much of your content as possible is available as HTML, especially links. If your links or navigation are rendered as images like GIFs or JPEGs, or if your site contains a lot of navigation in Flash, it will tend to be less accessible. Unless you have an HTML equivalent of this content, search engine crawlers will have a hard time indexing your stuff.

Most blogging tools will deal with all these issues for you. Generally, blogs consist of very well formed HTML and are very accessible to search engines. Plus they tend, by their very nature, to be very interlinked with other websites although the key here is that the links of value to you are links from others to your site, often called back links. It is worth restating that the best way of getting these kinds of links is to be interesting, useful or relevant to another blogger, combined with some of the more manual, or traditional marketing approaches to getting your site known, as follows.

8.3 Manual promotion

Networking

The primary and best way to reach an audience is to do some old-fashioned networking with bloggers you admire, read and with whom you share an interest. Take time to write to those individuals and wear your heart on your sleeve by blog rolling them. With any of the manual methods it may pay dividends to think through your tactics. You should target other weblogs carefully. The temptation is to find a popular, high-traffic site like Glenn Reynolds' Instapundit, 'US politics niche owner'.

While a link to your site from theirs will be invaluable, there are a good many bloggers out there with the same idea. The owners of that site will be inundated with requests to link, only a few of which will succeed. It will almost certainly pay greater dividends to identify other sites which maybe don't have such high traffic, but that do share some kind of interest with yours. In either case, when you make contact, don't beg for a link, but demonstrate your shared interest or at least offer some titbit tailored to the interest of your target.

A good place to look for leads for new contacts is your own referral log. The savvy blogger will read their referrals – the record of in-bound traffic – and study them for potential sites to develop a relationship with, to blogroll or monitor for interesting content. The super-savvy blogger will start with the lowest and newest referrers first. These are the guys who might love to create reciprocal links, they might even regard it as an honour. Certainly, contact with them is going to register on their radar much more than contact with the heavy-hitters. So, read your referrals and check the lower echelons first.

Instapundit – www.instapundit.com – Glenn Reynolds' massively popular, Washington politics commentary weblog

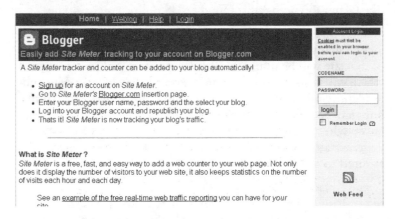

SiteMeter – www.sitemeter.com – Check the logs! Blogger users may want to consider a site visitor statistics tool like SiteMeter

Link and link again

It cannot be overstated: the key to successful weblogging is to enmesh yourself in the Web by linking. Remember, that if the other guys are smart they'll be seeing your site come up as a referrer to theirs and that will have a big impact. At the very least they'll wheel by your site to check you out. That's traffic!

The trackback system is designed to facilitate this. In effect, you're leaving a link to your site by creating a trackback on someone else's. Don't abuse it. Don't create blind trackback, where the link just leads to your site, with no reference to the original. Be interesting and relevant, add comment or celebrate a sentiment or observation of another. Bear in mind the total experience of a reader travelling from one site to yours. Will they get something new from your trackback? And target trackback to those who'll appreciate it. Again, find those interesting backwaters that might have been overlooked. At the very least you're likely to gain friends and readers from the authors of those sites.

A good tip is to follow the links on your site. Use your own weblog and its blogroll in particular as a portal to other sites. By doing this, you'll ramp up referrer logs on the other sites which again will get you noticed by their authors.

Another way of getting your site noticed on other blogs is to contribute comments to them. Just make sure you remember to include the URL or your own blog in the comment or as a link from your name. Similarly, you can target message boards or forums that operate in your fields of interest and contribute comment to them too. In both cases, take care to make your comments relevant and interesting or witty or challenging, not just a simple link to your site and a lame invitation to visit some time. Such comments are your calling card and are only worth doing if you're going to put a bit of effort in and represent yourself properly, by thinking of the context in which they appear. The absolute essential is not to beg for attention, but command it by genuinely engaging with the topic, discussion or point at hand. Better no link at all than a shameless appeal for traffic.

Real world marketing

Make sure you promote your URL wherever you promote yourself. You might consider having printed material created – business cards can be particularly effective – which promotes you and your blog. Extend that thought to a letterhead, flyers, T-shirts – you name it!

CaféPress – www.cafepress.com – design some merchandise to promote your blog, produce and retail via the CaféPress service

Product development

A key component of any marketing effort is to always think about your product, your blog, and how you could improve your offer to your readers. There are key issues of quality, pithiness and regularity of your posts. Are you trying to better your offer? Can you look at others you admire and use their ideas or approaches as inspiration?

If you're serious about growing your audience, you'll quickly become aware of the crowded nature of the marketplace. Therefore you'll need to refine your product, make it do what no other blog or website can do. This is partly about finding your voice, after all, there's no one else quite like you out there, but also it's about finding your niche and positioning yourself in relation to other sites, large and small, that deal with that topic or area of interest. For example, you could make your site about keeping tropical fish – but if you want to publish in the micro-niche of Oscar Fish keeping, know that you're going up against An Oscar Fish Blog!

An Oscar Fish Blog www.an-oscar-fish-blog.blogspot.com. The highly competitive micro-niche of Oscar Fish blogging

If you can make your site the definitive place for all the latest gossip or cutting-edge thinking on a certain subject or sub-division of a subject then you stand a good chance of making an impact. Otherwise, is there something missing in the blogs that deal with your favourite topics? Is there a new angle on a subject, does your unique voice add something which readers will find refreshing and insightful. It may be that you have much humbler aspirations and you just want to make the best site you can for your school or workplace. Even so, you should think about how your group relates to the world and therefore the Web. Are there educational issues you can follow and offer practical insight from the ground? What market is your company operating in? What issues and developments are interesting in the industry?

Whatever you choose to blog about, it pays to observe your position in relation to other related sites. Make sure you manage relations with both the big, high traffic sites 'upstream' of yours and the smaller or equivalent sites 'downstream'. The upstream sites will be happy to have an affiliate site which oversees a slice of a subject, and will start to look to you as an authority on the micro subject. Similarly, others on the same or lower levels to you in the blog pecking order will be very happy if you recognize them and trade links. The main thing to remember is: be different, plough a distinctive furrow and you will find a loyal and appreciative audience.

Summary

- Take advantage of automated tools to promote your site like Ping and RSS.

- Optimize your blog and posts for search engine recognition.

- Swap reciprocal ads with other sites.

- Build networks – read and contribute to other blogs and public forums to let people know you're there.

- Work out how your blog fits into the landscape of related sites and exploit the position fully.

- Link, link, link!

- Use real-world marketing devices such as business cards or T-shirts.

- Above all, make your blog the best it can be!

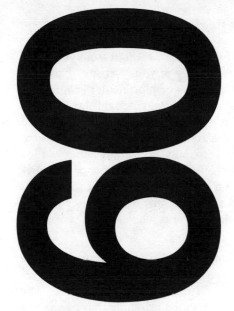

09

the distribution network

In this chapter you will learn:

- what syndication is
- about RSS and how it is useful
- about syndication feed systems
- how you and your readers can consume feeds
- how to integrate other feeds into your site

9.1 What is syndication?

Syndication is the process of sending out content from your blog so it can be consumed independently of your website. This may be on someone else's site, via a news or blog reader program or even in email or on a cell phone. You may be familiar with the concept of syndication from other media like newspapers and television. In the press, columns and cartoons are often syndicated to a number of publications, usually non-competing as they operate in different territories. Similarly in television, particularly in the United States, there is a market for the syndication of hit shows which have achieved a high volume of episodes, for local affiliate stations of the national networks who can then repeatedly schedule them.

Both these models are commercial and the owners of the syndicated content receive payment for their use by the re-publishers or broadcasters. In the gift economy of the blogosphere, syndication works on the principle that by sharing some of your content you will reap a reward in terms of greater exposure and therefore traffic to your site. It is worth bearing in mind that syndication of weblog content is in your control. You can elect to syndicate some or none of your posts, but whatever you syndicate will always contain links back to your site.

What is RSS and Atom?

Ever wondered what those little orange buttons were, you know the ones marked with the letters 'RSS' and 'XML' and 'ATOM'? Well here's your two minute catch-up on some arcane weblore!

RSS stands for a number of things. Really Simple Syndication, Rich Site Summary or RDF (Resource Description Framework) Site Summary. The reason there are differing definitions is that, for historical reasons, RSS has a number of versions. RSS was originally developed by Netscape who abandoned it once they were taken over by AOL. Dave Winer at Radio Userland took up the cudgels for RSS and acquired rights to the code then developed the standard as part of the Userland blog service. You can recognize the ownership of Userland RSS by looking out for the versions of RSS numbered 0.9x and 2.0. However, RSS

Feed Icons – www.feedicons.com – is attempting to create a new standard button to do away with the many different RSS version numbers, ATOM, and XML buttons.

branched when Userland took proprietary ownership, as another group of engineers decided to describe a more complex, although more open, standard and they called that version 1.0.

Just to complicate matters further, another group of software developers introduced an additional RSS-like standard which is known as Atom. This standard has been adopted by Blogger as the house standard for syndication. Atom has more in common with RSS 1.0 than Userland's 2.0, in that it is a more complex but more stable standard, although its introduction and widespread adoption has led to some suggestions that the time is right to re-unify the different strands of development into a single, über-standard.

Unless you are interested in developing software widgets to read RSS or Atom feeds, it is not really essential to know this stuff. For the content publisher and consumer, you just need to know that it works. However, just to de-mystify the notion of RSS, it might be worth looking at the structure of a basic RSS document, so you can see how Really Simple it is!

It uses a language called XML (Extensible Mark-up Language) to describe news headlines and news-like content, although it could be used to describe pretty much anything.

Unlike HTML which was originally – and in some ways still is – a formatting language, XML is a language to describe data structures. An RSS document always starts with a definition of the version that is in use. This declaration will often look something like <rss version ="2.0">. The most common tags are <channel>, <title>, <description>, <link> and <language>. Within each <channel> tag there are usually a number of <item> tags which in themselves are further defined by <title> and <description>.

The RSS document itself is simply a text document with the file extension .rss.

If you're using a very basic or home-brew system to create your weblog, you can hand-code RSS documents in a text editor, and publish them on your site. The purpose of sharing the above breakdown is not intended as a recommendation that you do it. If you're using a hosted system like Blogger or Typepad then such things are done automatically by the system. All you and your audience need to do, is to subscribe!

9.2 Consuming feeds

Now you've got the principles and an insight into some of the technical approaches to syndication, lets look at the benefits of all this to the end-user: people like you and me who haven't got the time to go crawling through our bookmarks to see who's updated their site and who hasn't. What we need is some help with all these sites and their syndication feeds. What we need are news aggregators. These are also known as news readers, RSS readers, feed readers or feed aggregators.

However they're referred to, all these are programs which are primarily designed to save time and effort keeping up to speed with the websites that you're interested in. In effect, what they allow you to do is create a dynamic, personal web-collage – one that's made up of all the best and most relevant bits of all the different sites that are lucky enough to count you as a reader.

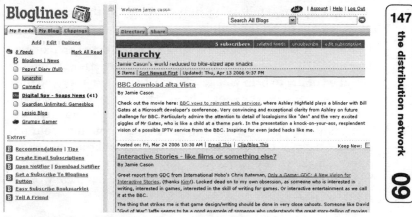

Feeds can bring together the best from many blogs

There's a massive choice of news aggregators out there, but they all provide the same basic functions.

1 They let you subscribe to feeds. This is where those funny orange buttons on people's sites come in. Right-click on the button, select **Copy Shortcut** from the drop-down menu, then paste the link to your news aggregator's new subscription box. A lot of aggregators will also support searches for feeds. Once you've found and saved a link in the aggregator, the program knows you're interested in that site and will keep tabs on it for you.

2 Once you've subscribed, the news aggregator will automatically 'pull' the content of the feed – as we've seen, usually a title, a summary or first line and a link at least. It will do this at regular intervals, which you can usually adjust within the program.

3 When it has retrieved an updated feed, it will often have some means of alerting you that hot news is breaking.

4 When you launch the program it will then display the feed for you within its own interface. Remember that it will just be the summary of the post – the pure essence stripped of any formatting, ads and usually, though not always, pictures, from the host site.

5 The interface shows you all the feeds from all your subscribed sites in one place and allows you to quickly consume the

latest updates, following links through to the main sites if you want to get the full deal.

Certainly, if you're a regular visitor to more than three or four websites you can see how this simple, yet powerful technology could be of use to help you get the most out of your online time. And as a publisher, you should be able to see the benefit of giving away summaries in syndication in order to facilitate your readers' consumption of your stuff. You should also note that your aim is to get them to follow that link, so the age-old rules of content apply – make your post useful, relevant and take time to 'sell' it in the title, as this is the teaser that's going to be out there working hard for you.

9.3 Choosing a news aggregator

One of the other common factors about news aggregators is that they tend to be free. There are also an awful lot of them available for use or download on the Web. This massive amount of choice can be very confusing. The tool you choose will be dependent on the kind of operating system you're running, usually either Windows or Macintosh. The next thing to consider is whether you'd like to use an online or offline tool.

Online tools

Rather like a lot of the popular weblogging systems, some of the news aggregation tools available run through your web browser and are accessible via a website. Examples of systems like this are BlogLines (www.bloglines.com), 24eyes (www.24eyes.com) and Yahoo! (my.yahoo.com). Most of these kinds of services are free, and some require registration in order to save your preferences. They all offer differing ways of managing subscriptions and different ways of viewing and consuming content. Their key benefit is that, as they are online, you can access them from any computer.

Some, like Bloglines, offer a downloadable component that will periodically check for updates to your subscriptions while your computer is online, and alert you to changes. The online systems also work well if you are running an 'always on' connection like

DSL or cable, as alerts can happen without having to trigger a dial-up and disturb you all over again. Some web services like Yahoo! are integrating news reading capability into their offer, so you can set up your subscriptions alongside other services that they provide.

NewsGator (www.newsgator.com) offer a free Web-based RSS aggregator

Offline tools

Also known as desktop tools, these are programs that need to be downloaded and installed on your machine. You set them up and use them in a very similar way to the online tools, creating and managing subscriptions, but the key difference is that while the software will still need access to the Internet to download the content for you, once it is downloaded you can browse it offline. Some examples of these kinds of programs are Amphetadesk, RSSOwl, NetNewsWire (for Macintosh only) and FeedDemon (for Windows, also combines the functions of an online and offline tool). Most of the popular web browsers including Explorer, Safari, Firefox and Opera now also support some form of feed reading.

You can also download plug-ins, extra bits of software for email client programs like Outlook and the key benefit to the offline tools is that they will allow you to consume content, to a certain degree depending on how much they download for you, while disconnected from the Internet. This is perfect if you're going to be on the move but still want to be able to keep up with your favourite sources of news. It does mean that you'll have to schedule some online time to go and get all that new content though. Significantly, there is also a large range of newsreading software for cell or mobile phones which enables direct download or browsing on these portable devices.

9.4 Podcasting

The term 'podcast' is a hybrid of 'iPod' and 'broadcast' and seeks to define a new way of distributing rich media content, beyond broadcasting. The phenomenon of podcasting has extended the principles of RSS/Atom and the syndication of content to audio and increasingly, video as well. A straight-forward text and image blogging has revolutionized web and print publishing, and like public access cable did before it, so podcasting has created a whole bunch of home-brew radio and TV stars who now have a route to an audience which was previously controlled by TV and radio networks.

In this field, the biggest aggregator of content is iTunes. This is not the only way of doing it, but Apple have made it easy and therefore they dominate. They have seamlessly integrated the iPod hardware with the synchronization function of iTunes software on your Mac or PC and by extension the online iTunes Music Store. By making that process so easy for the end user, Apple has established a very strong position in the market. If you're creating your own audio/visual content (what we used to call TV and radio shows!) then you could use iTunes, possibly via a deal with an affiliate like Audible.com, to reach an audience. Unless you're an established name, this will probably be given away free.

If you're making video, you might also look at services like Google Video. This is an open system for contributors, although a proprietary system for consumers in that you either have to stream the video from the Google site or if you want to download it, you need to use the Google video player. Services like Google Video and YouTube offer a tremendously powerful platform for finding an audience if VOD (Video On Demand) casting is your thing. All this said, many of the blogging services are starting to offer, certainly as part of their premium packages, ways of presenting audio and video content in your blog and allowing your visitors ways of subscribing to, and automatically downloading, new content. This in effect creates a pod or VODcast equivalent. All you need to do is make interesting, relevant, great content!

Download podcasts – or add your own – at PodCast (www.podcast.net)

Summary

- Help to retain a loyal reader base by syndicating your content via RSS or Atom feeds.

- Get yourself a news aggregator to keep track of all the blogs you're interested in.

- Bypass traditional media outlets to podcast your own audio or video show.

10 managing contributors

In this chapter you will learn:

- how to deal with comment/ TrackBack spam

- how to deal with genuine contributors

- how to blog with others

- how to set and maintain standards

10.1 Many pieces loosely joined

One way or another blogging is a collaborative effort. Although a very loosely joined confederation, if you blog, you are part of a global community of bloggers. You've all put yourself out there, taken a risk and you will all have familiar stories of dealing with publishing software, favourite posts that you have written and read, inevitable struggles to keep the blog going, and you'll all have tales of contributors, wanted and unwanted.

Enabling feedback on your posts

There are two ways of managing feedback from your readers. If you enable *comments*, you allow your readers to publish their thoughts on your post. Sometimes a contentious or interesting post will spark a long discussion with several participants – including yourself of course – leaving comments. And sometimes the discussion will go round in circles or veer off in a direction you see no future in, and you may decide you want to put a stop to it. This is your blog, and you say when enough is enough! At this point you can edit the post and change the comments setting.

These are at the bottom of the posting window in most blogging tools – click **Post & Comment Options** in Blogger to show the options. Set **Comments** to **None** (TypePad) or **No & Hide Existing** (Blogger), which displays no comments at all. Or set it to **Closed** (TypePad) or **No** (Blogger) which displays the discussion to date – but prevents anyone from adding any more to it.

Trackbacks are the second feedback method: Blogger calls them *Backlinks*. It is a bit like commenting, but instead of readers posting their comments on your blog, they publish them as posts on their own blogs, and link them back to your post (see box on the next page for more on this). When saving a post you can decide whether to allow people to link their posts to yours in this way. To allow trackbacks in TypePad, tick the **Accept TrackBacks** checkbox. You can also link this post to someone else's post by sending your own TrackBack to it (you will need their TrackBack address to do this, which you'll find on their post if they have enabled it). In Blogger, you have the same options to allow trackbacks as you do with comments: **Yes** to allow, **No** to block new trackbacks (but show any existing ones) or **No &** **Hide Existing** to suppress all trackbacks.

TrackBack

Also known as PingBack, TrackBack is a protocol first specified by SixApart in their Movable Type software, but now adopted by many other blogging services. If blogger one writes a new post which comments on a post on another blog (let's call it 'blog two'), and both the blogging systems support TrackBack, then the original post from blog two will be alerted to the fact that blogger one has commented over on their blog. Blog two will automatically publish a list of other blogs that have commented on theirs. The idea is to facilitate cross-fertilization between blogs, to enable reader journeys between different weblogs by following conversations linked by TrackBack.

You should consider disallowing comments and TrackBacks on older entries in your weblog. The older the entry, the more spam it will collect. It becomes like a honey-pot for spam engines and scripts.

10.2 Combating spam

Unfortunately, the most common experience that bloggers will have of contributors is undesirable. The direct cause of this trouble is not even human but its source is all too human. This is the scourge of comment and TrackBack *spam*.

Combating this is a chore. You'll have to think of it like house-keeping. In any house you have chores to do which maintain the fabric of the place and your standards of cleanliness and hygiene. Some houses need a light dusting from time to time, some are infested with giant 'roaches. So it is with comment and TrackBack spam.

What is spam?

Most people are familiar with the unwanted, unsolicited email in their inbox known as spam. Like computer viruses, spam is one of the negative products of the Internet and the communication traffic between machines attached to the network.

Geek fact #1: origins of spam

Spam gets its name from the Monty Python sketch set in a café which serves nothing but dishes featuring the processed pork product: Spam. The repetition of the word in the sketch is a similar effect to the overload of useless information that junk up our lives.

Spam is a form of direct marketing and a fairly incomprehensible one at that, given that the products and services promoted therein are pretty specialist to say the least. Because of the low cost of creating and distributing email in massive bulk, there is no financial barrier to sending messages to hundreds of thousands of utterly random email addresses. Lists of email addresses are collected and traded for the purposes of spam. The collection of email often happens automatically by similar programs to those which index the Internet on behalf of search engines. These are programs known as 'bots (short for robots), which crawl webpages in search of email addresses.

Protect your email address

Blogs can often, unwittingly, be a rich harvest of email addresses for software which trawls the Web looking for items to add to spam lists. This is why you see email addresses disguised or rendered non-machine readable so as to be overlooked by the spam bots. This is sometimes referred to as 'munging' details. It is definitely advisable to do this yourself if you're publishing your email address on your site or anyone else's. There are a number of ways of doing this. Here are a few examples.

If your address is usually written in the form:

yourname@yourdomain.com

then try writing out your address in this way:

yourname at yourdomain dot com

or

yourname_at_yourdomain_dot_com

Alternatively you can write it out in a human-readable sentence like: My email address ends with 'yourdomain.com' and begins with 'yourname' separated by an 'at' symbol.

With blogs there is another, altogether more annoying way you can be spammed. The 'bots create comments or trackback links on your posts. This can be done directly by humans too, but if you're in the business of spamming, you've usually got some software employees out there doing it for you in an industrialized way, hitting thousands of sites at a time. The comments themselves can look innocent enough; they might contain text such as 'Nice site!' or more straight-forwardly, an advertising message and a link back to the contributor's site. The site that's linked is usually for a business of some kind, it might be offensive or pornographic, which can often add insult to the injury of clogging up your lovely blog with nonsense comments.

Sneakily, the bogus comment might link to an otherwise normal looking blog. The main benefit for comment/trackback spammers is that by creating a lot of links to their sites, their sites will rank higher in search engines. It doesn't matter whether you or a visitor to your site follows the link, the fact that the search engine thinks that *you* think the site is relevant by linking to it, is enough incentive.

Combating comment and trackback spam

You can always turn off the comments and trackback features on your blog posts (most services will let you set 'off' as the default setting), but this undermines the whole ethos of blogging. The links between like-minded blogs are what makes the blogosphere so special. Most blogging software systems recognize comment and trackback spam as being of very serious concern to their subscribers and all are therefore, keen to add features to their systems and to support broader web standards that might help to control the incidence of spam.

The main innovation in this area as far as reducing the effectiveness of comment and trackback spam to increase search engine results, is the introduction of the <rel="nofollow"> tag descriptor for any links added by a contributor to a blog. This code tells Search Engines not to count this link when calculating page rank, therefore removing the point of comment spam for the spammers. A standard user need not worry too much about this code, as it is automatically added by most blogging software, including Typepad and Blogger, when it builds your page. The unfortunate side-effect is that genuine contributors don't receive a benefit for their addition to your site, by getting a boost for their own site in search engines.

Word verification

Two of the best ways of fighting comment spam are based on foiling automated software agents, this means verifying that a contributor is human before their comment can be added. Blogger achieves this by offering a word verification system. In this process, a contributor must read a word or set of characters published in a machine-unreadable format – images of wobbly stretched letters with odd lines and bars through them – then retype what they see before their comment will be accepted. This is also known as a 'captcha' system.

Geek fact #2: captcha and Turing tests

'Captcha' is a terribly strained acronym, perhaps invented by someone very tired after a long night's creative programming – it stands for Completely Automated Public Turing test to tell Computers and Humans Apart. Alan Turing is a kind of godfather of digital computing theory, and he proposed a test which would determine the boundary between computer and human intelligence. It's actually nothing like the captcha word verification test, but Turing carries a great deal of geek cachet.

This is a tried and trusted means of authentication, and in the Blogger system this can be applied on a comment by comment basis. To use word verification in Blogger you should go to the **Settings | Comments** tab and click the **Yes** button to activate it.

Blogger's word verification system

You can always go back to this screen later and turn it off again if you decide you don't want to use it.

This is taken a step further by TypeKey. Their system allows users to prove themselves as humans once, by creating a TypeKey account, and then use their TypeKey identity as an automatic authentication system whenever they want to add comments to any blog which supports the TypeKey standard. The method used to demonstrate your humanity is similar to Blogger's word verification, in that at registration you have to retype a sequence of characters published in machine-unreadable form. The TypeKey system is administered by Typepad, but is offered as an open standard so that other blogging tools can freely integrate it in their systems.

These kinds of authentication only work for you if you turn them on though! If you do, they will stop virtually all scripted and automated comment spamming engines.

In TypePad you can set your **Weblog Comment Preferences** so that comment authentication is required.

If set to **Required**, then your visitors must first create or login to an existing TypeKey account prior to submitting a comment. If it is set to **Optional** users can submit comments without first logging into TypeKey.

Using TypeKey authentication in TypePad

Removing spam from your site

If you decide not to use the authentication systems described above, or your publishing system doesn't support them, then spam may still get through. If it does, then you can simply delete the comment by using the normal administration features. This is the kind of house-keeping chore that you'll need to keep up. If you leave spam unattended, it does tend to attract more spam as the spam scripts return to places where they learn that their messages will persist.

TypePad encourage you to report spam in order that they can implement system-wide efforts to prevent it. To assist in this effort, make sure you select all of the comment details before deleting the comment and copy them so that they can be pasted into a report. To do this in TypePad use **List TrackBacks** in the **List Comments** tab of your Weblogs administration area, then select the checkbox next to the comment or trackback you want to mark as spam. Use the **Delete as Junk** button to delete the comment or trackback from your weblog, and paste in the text of the comment or trackback in your report to TypePad.

Deleting Trackback spam in TypePad

Banning IP addresses

If you're troubled by a persistent spammer, you can ban the commenter's IP address. In TypePad use the TypePad Control Panel to ban an IP from commenting on your site. The spammers frequently change IPs with their messages so this is not always helpful but it can help if you are receiving messages from the same IP.

10.3 Moderation

Some forms of managing contributors are good for handling human and automated contributors. Blogger and TypePad both support forms of comment and trackback moderation. This keeps spam and other unwanted content from being published automatically to your weblog because you must approve all comments and trackback before they are published. In both cases you need to activate the systems on your blog.

If you're a TypePad user, go to the Comment and Trackback Preferences section, select the **Notify** checkbox and save the setting. This will notify you, in any case, when new material is contributed. Furthermore, you can choose to hold comments and trackback for approval. You may find that TypePad automatically deletes a comment or trackback that it has identified as spam. It does this by checking against reports from other users, and does your moderation for you!

>> Comment and TrackBack Preferences

Hold comments and TrackBacks for approval? ☐ NEW
If selected, all comments submitted to this weblog will not be published until they have been approved.

Activating comment approval in TypePad

In Blogger you can use a similar system by going to the **Settings | Comments** tab where you can enable comment moderation via a Yes or No radio button. You'll then be prompted to add the email address at which you wish to be notified when a new comment is posted.

Unreviewed Comments (Sort: Post Name, Comment Date)   Comments per page: 50 ▾

Select: All None

PUBLISH	REJECT		1 - 2 of 2
☐ ↖ Is it time for tea yet? Publish Reject		(Arthur Dent)	12:07 PM
☐ ▶ hi		(kimmy)	11:13 AM
PUBLISH	REJECT		1 - 2 of 2

Select: All None

Using comment moderation in Blogger

For real contributors, do think carefully about your use of moderation. It will be better for you and the development of your site if you use it wisely and as sparingly as possible. Remember that contributors to your site are likely to be very loyal visitors, if only to see how you react to them. They are also likely to be opinionated and may express themselves in a different way from you. Just because you may disagree with someone, or you may not like their style, it isn't always the best idea to simply delete their post. Or if they publish a comment at odds with your position, then you post a blisteringly aggressive riposte. Contributors need to be treated with respect and nurtured, even if you disagree.

Remember also that readers not involved in the conversation will be very sensitive to how you deal with contributors, no matter how pig-headed they are. Most fair-minded observers will be able to take a balanced view in a discussion and their opinion of you will be much more positive if you stay reasonable and polite in your dealings with visitors. What if these folks came over to your house? How would you behave if you were hosting a party? The nicer you play it, the nicer your guests will be. But if you're always spoiling for a fight, then that's likely what you'll get! Or worse, left on your own, punching air.

10.4 House rules and editorial guidelines

Everyone has different thresholds of what is acceptable on their site. You almost certainly have a set of standards for yourself, even if these only exist in your head. In any case there need to be limits. This applies to topic, tone, language and style. Most bloggers write fairly informally. The main authors on the blog will tend to set the agenda with what they choose to post about and how much they solicit comment by asking questions of readers in their posts. The tone of most blogs tends to be friendly, even joshing, and it is unusual for blogs to publish detailed rules for contributors.

Having said that, you might want to consider writing down some of your unwritten standards, especially if your blog gets popular. What's your position on adult humour and language? Will you tolerate racism, homophobia or sexism? What about jargon and txt spk? If you find yourself having to moderate a lot of comment, it is very good to be able to be as consistent in your editorial decisions as possible. While being moderated can inflame contributors, there's nothing worse than a contributor who's inflamed *and* has a sense of righteous injustice.

If you choose to blog with friends or colleagues, it is good to have a formal, shared sense of what your blog is about and some rules about what kind of material is acceptable on the site. Not only will it help you to present a more consistent and rewarding experience to your readers, it will also help as a touchstone for discussing the direction for the site.

Rules and guidelines can cover as much about the site as you think is necessary, from when to use upper case letters to defining that all posts must stay on a particular topic. The kinds and quantity of rules that you have will vary to suit you, but the key thing where you share authorship of a blog is that all the authors also buy in to the ideals embodied in the guidelines. It might be worthwhile thinking about periods of review where you take a look at the rules, to see if they're working or still relevant and agree any new rules or changes to the old ones. The main thing is to maintain a consensus and understanding across your team.

Multiple authors

Many blog publishing systems offer the ability to invite and permit multiple authors. Often this functionality is packaged in the premium products offered by the hosting provider. You need to consider this requirement when setting up your blog, but if things change later, it is relatively easy to upgrade your product or move to a system that supports multiple authors.

TypePad

In TypePad you need to have a Pro account in order to invite multiple authors. If they aren't already a TypePad account holder, they'll be offered a free guest account when they receive your invitation. According to how much moderating control you wish to have over the contributor, you can set their permissions as either a junior or guest author. Junior authors can post drafts that you as the site owner will need to review and publish and they cannot publish images or other files. Guest authors have added privileges in that their posts can be published to your weblog, and they can upload photos and files to the weblog, without your approval or intervention each time.

Blogger

In Blogger, there are two levels of privilege:

- An **Admin** member will have all the same privileges as you, the blog owner, in that they can change the settings of the blog, add, edit and delete posts made by all team members.

- **Non-Admin** team members only have the ability to post. You can set team members as Administrators by checking the box next to their name in the **Settings | Members** tab.

Very high-end users of TypePad, with Business Class Accounts, can set up multiple Administrators who can share in the administrative functions of the weblog. This is a position of great trust and privilege and should not be handed out lightly. It is most beneficial if you are sharing a relatively large-scale, corporate-style weblog for your place of work or school, where it is necessary that more than one person have these responsibilities in case of absence or changes in personnel. This will prevent the weblog becoming 'locked' if a single administrator can't attend to their duties for a period of time.

How to set up multiple authors

TypePad

It is easy here to set-up new authors to post on your weblog.

1 Follow the **Edit Configuration** link on the **Weblogs** tab for the particular weblog you want to add the author to, then click the **Authors** link to open the Weblog Authors setup page.

2 In the **Invite Additional Authors to your Weblog** area, enter the name and email address for the author you would like to invite. Remember, you can invite more than one at a time, just list their names and email addresses within this form. You can enter a covering message with the invitation, or use the default message provided.

3 Once you're ready, click **Send Invitation** at the bottom of the page and your guest will receive an email invitation to join your weblog. The status of their invitation is shown under

Open Invitations. If you wish you can also cancel the invitation from here.

Blogger

In Blogger, multiple author blogs are known as Team Blogs. If you're a Blogger user you can set up a Team Blog via the **Members** tab under the **Settings** menu heading.

1 Once you hit the **Add Team Members** button, you'll get a form where you can enter multiple email addresses for those blogging pals you'd like to invite.

2 If the invitees don't already have a Blogger account they'll be invited to create one, and you get an email notification when they accept your invitation.

Managing authors

From time to time, you may wish to amend the privileges or access of your multiple authors or team members.

Blogger

Under the **Settings > Members** tab you can change admin status using the **Admin?** checkboxes and if you want to remove a team member, then just check the box in the **Remove** column next to their name.

TypePad

Under the **Current Authors** heading on the Weblog Authors page, the authors for the weblog are listed along with their access level. Here, you can change the access level for the author, or remove an author from the weblog by clicking the trash can icon next to the author name.

Summary

- ◆ Comments and TrackBack are an essential part of creating the rich world of the blogosphere.

  Comment and TrackBack spam is an unwanted nuisance: combat it using spam-prevention tools on your blogging service.

  Be prepared to have to tidy up your blog from time to time to remove any spam which still gets through.

  Use the ability to moderate comments on your blog sparingly.

  When writing with other authors, agree house rules and editorial guidelines early, and review them regularly.

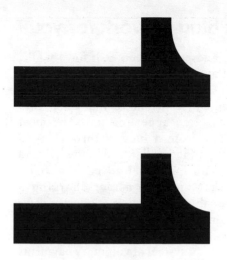

blogging for profit

In this chapter you will learn:

- how blogs can work for you financially
- how to earn money from advertising
- about subscription and donation models
- about other potential sources of income

11.1 Putting your blog to work for you

If you're blogging properly, and you've been at it for a while, then your blog will embody a great deal of hard work on your part. For most bloggers this is a labour of love and you won't begrudge it – but if you *can* convert some of that effort into financial reward, well that's often appealing too. The most common way to earn money from a blog is through paid advertising, usually by participating in a large ad network, and occasionally through deals with individual advertisers. Blogs operating in a niche market might consider charging a subscription for access to valuable information – industry news from a well-placed source, for instance. This is quite rare in the gift economy of the blogosphere, however, and should not be adopted lightly. More common is a system of voluntary payments or donations: if you like my blog, help support it by leaving a small tip.

Then there are the blog spin-offs: your collected posts might be turned into a book or a photo library with real commercial value; you might offer T-shirts and other merchandise for sale, so that followers of your cult ramblings can mark their space with your brand. You should probably not start off your blog with these at the forefront of your mind though, as they're only remotely feasible if your blog turns out to be a really popular site – and even then it's going to take some time.

Corporate and other non-personal blogs

Finally, there are indirect ways in which bloggers can bring home the bacon through a corporate blog, or a blog about the football team or band you play in. Many companies are starting to use blogs as a way of building up a buzz about their products, and of keeping in touch with their customers' wants and needs. The informal atmosphere of a blog, the way readers are encouraged to join in with comments and trackbacks, is ideal for this purpose – and very cost-effective compared with traditional marketing.

And if you are blogging on behalf of a group or organization which you are part of, you can use this space as a way of letting your fans know about gigs or fixtures. Are you holding a bring-

and-buy sale to raise funds for the Twiddleton Tiddlywinks Club? Post it on your blog! Come Monday morning, when eager supporters log on to the TTC blog to check up on the week's league results, they can put it in their diaries and help ensure a good turn-out.

11.2 Advertising

As with other media, one way of deriving income from a website is to charge advertisers for the privilege of placing their promotional material next to your original content. Your hard work has established a sizable and regular readership, and you can sell this fact to people who want to sell their products and services to these people. Moreover, most successful blogs have a niche of their own, attracting a very particular kind of audience. This enables advertisers to direct their ads towards exactly the kind of people most likely to respond (*content targeting*), which they will be willing to pay a premium for.

Arranging your own advertising

If you are with a blogging service provider you will generally find that there are restrictions on paid advertising content. For instance, Blogger's advertising program is run by Google, whose rules forbid the appearance of any competing ads on the same page as their ads. If you host your blog on your own webspace, you are free to do pretty much whatever you like in terms of slapping adverts all over your site. All you have to do is find the advertisers, make the deals, ensure the necessary technical infrastructure is in place to track the data, put the ads on your page, prepare reports for the advertisers, issue invoices and chase up non-payers, manage the expectations and frustrations of irate advertising execs when you fail to deliver on your promised traffic figures ... Still want to go it alone?!

Advertising the easy way

The alternative is to just sign up for an advertising network. You won't have to deal with any negotiations over terms and prices, or sort out any technical issues such as ad-views or click-throughs. The network will do all of that for you – and take a slice of the action in return. This arrangement works well for everyone. You only have to fill in a form or two; the advertisers only have to deal with one point of contact to arrange large-scale advertising (across many small sites); and the network makes a small amount of money off each of a large number of sites. The only people who might lose out in this kind of scheme are really high-profile bloggers who know they can command higher advertising fees if they move outside the standard structures.

Many blogging services offer their own advertising programs which are ideal for most bloggers. Blogger uses its parent company Google's AdSense scheme; TypePad partners the Kanoodle network. In both cases, they offer an easy route to getting signed up with a well-established network which runs content-targeted advertising.

Using AdSense with Blogger

AdSense is Google's scheme for placing targeted content on a wide network of (generally) smallish sites. You can set up an AdSense account and link it to your blog from your Blogger account.

1   Log in and click **Template**, then **AdSense**. Make sure the contact and language settings are right, then read the **Terms and Conditions**, tick the box and hit **Create Account.**

2   This will send a confirmation email to the email address you specified, which you need to reply to in order to finish setting up the account. Check your email and follow the link given in it to the AdSense application form.

3   You'll be asked for a password and contact details, including a payee name for cheques. Over the next few days, your site will be checked over to ensure it complies with their editorial guidelines on acceptable sites. This means no gambling, pornography or hate content, no drug, alcohol, tobacco or weapons promotion, not too much profanity or other advertising, and no sneaky tricks to try to cheat site visitors, search engines or advertisers!

Signing up for an AdSense account

4 Assuming you meet the guidelines, you'll get an email confirming that you've been signed up and you'll start receiving ads on your blog shortly after that. You will also need to log into your AdSense account and set up payment information (including tax details, to comply with US tax law – this is a US company) before you can receive any money.

5 Back at Blogger, you should now be looking at a preview of your blog with some ads on it, and you can choose from a number of sample layouts and colour schemes to find something you're happy with. If none of the preset colour schemes suits you, there is a **Custom** option which allows you to set colours for each component of the ad using hex values (see page 107). You will see this preview screen whenever you return to the **Templates > AdSense** tab, and you can tinker with layout and colours at any time.

Setting a colour scheme for the AdSense ads in a Blogger blog

6 Click on the **AdSense Console** link just above the preview area to log into your account and check up on statistics – number of ads served, revenue earned, and so on.

Don't expect big bucks straight away. You earn very small amounts for each ad, and there's a minimum of $100 (at the time of writing) for the monthly cheque – if you have earned less than that threshold it is carried over into the next month.

Ads on TypePad

To join TypePad's advertising program you will need to have a Pro account.

1 Go to the **Control Panel** and click on **Earnings.** If you have not already set up an advertising account, hit the **Go to Setup** button – or go to the **Weblogs** tab, click **Design** and then choose **Change content selections.**

2 On this page, scroll down to the **Your SideBar Content** section to find **Text Ads** and click the **Configure** link. This opens a pop-up widow with two options: **Easy Setup** sets you up with

some default settings, or **Customize.** This gives you control over the number of ads displayed, the kind of products or services advertised, and the colours used.

3 When you're happy with your settings, tick the **Terms of Service** checkbox and click **Save Changes** to close the pop-up window. Now scroll down and hit **Save Changes** again to place the ads on your sidebar.

TypePad's advertising model is slightly different from Blogger's: it is a paid service, so it aims in the first place to pay off your subscription fees using advertising. So as long as your advertising revenues are less than your monthly subscription, you don't actually receive any money, you just get charged less for your blog. Once your earnings cross that threshold, they start to build up in your TypePad account. You can transfer money out of here into a PayPal account (and from there into a real-world account if you like), providing you have more than a certain minimum amount in credit ($15.01 at the time of writing). You will need to provide TypePad with some tax information before you can do this, in order to comply with US tax law.

To track your earnings, make withdrawals or edit income settings, go to the **Control Panel** and click on **Earnings**.

Using Google ads on TypePad

TypePad will also allow you to run Google ads in the sidebars, and you don't need a Pro account for this. Go to the TypeLists tab and add a new list of type 'Notes'. Then add a new Item, copying the ad code supplied by Google into the Note field.

11.3 Subscriptions and donations

If you host your own blog, you can restrict content to fee-paying subscribers, but this is not usually the case on hosted services such as Blogger or TypePad. Given the vast amount of information available free on the Internet, you also need to be in a very strong position to charge hard cash for access! A more viable model is to make some content available to all and then have a restricted, fee-paying area where you keep the really juicy gossip – but even then, you need to be very sure that you've got something worth paying for. Or perhaps if you're a podcaster you could bundle up a bunch of casts and burn them on to a 'greatest hits' CD. Then you're giving people something extra which they feel is worth paying for.

Another alternative is the donations or 'busker' model: basically you ask readers to throw you some small change if they like what they see. Or perhaps your blog has a campaigning element which you ask your readers to contribute to – you can collect donations on behalf of other organizations as well as yourself. To enable your audience to make what will generally be quite small donations, you will really need to use some kind of Internet-based payment mechanism such as PayPal. Unfortunately, setting up and running a PayPal account is beyond the scope of this book, but there is of course a low-tech alternative. Instead of enabling Internet-based payments, you could just give an address or some bank details and get people to send you cheques or bank transfers.

Are you worth it?

With both of these revenue models, you need first to ask yourself whether you are really worth paying to read? Without wanting to pour cold water on your sterling efforts, you have to place them in context. There is a huge amount of free material available online, and asking for money for anything which is not genuinely out of the ordinary is likely to be seen as plain cheeky! And even if your blog clearly is special, a little humility goes a long way – ask nicely and people might give. Scream 'SHOW ME THE MONEY!' and they are likely to raise their eyebrows and disappear, never to return.

TypePad's Tip Jar

TypePad formally incorporates the donations model into its offering – they call it the **Tip Jar**, and as with the ad scheme, it's only available to users with Pro membership or higher.

1   To enable your Tip Jar, go to the **Weblogs** tab, click **Design** and then choose **Change content selections**.

2   Scroll down to the **Tip Jar** and click **Configure** – this opens a pop-up window (see next page) with options for the size and wording of your request for donations – humble, remember! You can also link it to a post describing why you're asking for donations and what worthy cause, if any, you are collecting on behalf of.

11.4 Other potential sources of income

If you have a reasonably popular blog, the steady stream of small ad payments or donations may add up to a respectable sum, making it a hobby which pays for itself and a little more. Many bloggers dream of turning it into a full-time job which pays a living wage, or possibly even great riches. If you are one of these, here is a quick reality check. *Very few* people get paid to syndicate their content. *Even fewer* get that book deal. It does happen, but it is as much about being in the right place at the right time as having the soul of a super-blogger.

Configure Your Tip Jar

Modify your Tip Jar configuration and click the Save Changes button.

1 Select a Tip Jar Badge Style

Visitors to your site will click this badge to send you a tip.

○ 🍵 **Tip Jar** Change is good

○ 🍵 **Tip Jar** Change is good

○ **Tip Jar** Change is good

○ **Tip Jar** Change is good

○ TIP JAR THANK YOU!

◉ TIP JAR THANK YOU!

Customize your Tip Jar Badge

Title: Tip Jar   3 left

Description: Change is good   0 left

Enter a custom title and description for your Tip Jar.

Link to Post: No Post Link ▾

Add a link below your Tip Jar badge that points your visitors to a post on your weblog that describes your campaign.

2 Set a suggested Donation Amount (Optional)

Done   www.typepad.com

Configuring the Tip Jar at TypePad

Fortunately, you don't have to hang around waiting for other people to come and offer you money for your brain-dump. There are a number of ways you can take the initiative if you have an entrepreneurial nature.

Print on demand

Once upon a time, it took a massive amount of manpower to prepare a book for printing, and a vast array of unwieldy technology to put it onto paper – you had to be sure of selling a few thousand copies of the book to make it even worth considering. Then on top of that you've got the costs of marketing and selling the book – it won't ship itself to bookstores all on its lonesome. Digital printing technology and desktop publishing software now make it financially viable to print just a handful of copies, with minimal investment. Selling the book via your own website or on an e-marketplace such as eBay also entails practically no up-front costs. If you are convinced that the collected wisdom in a year's worth of blogging would make a great book for someone, you can work it up into a book format and sell it quietly online, printing only as many as are needed to fulfil the actual demand.

If nobody buys it, well all you've really lost is the time spent preparing the book – you don't need to stump up a couple of grand for printing and marketing and risk losing it all. If it proves to be a winner, you'll be making several pounds from each copy rather than the 10% of net you'd get if you went through a traditional publishing house. And if you wanted to, you'd then be in a strong position to take the work to a publisher. Having proved the concept, they are more likely to be willing to invest in the big marketing push you need to take your book from online cult success to the bestseller lists.

Merchandise

There's a T-shirt and a mouse mat for everything these days, so why not for your blog? As with paper publishing, the cost barriers to entry in these markets are virtually nil. There are merchandising companies who will produce very small numbers of items at low cost – you just supply the design to them. And again, there are plenty of e-commerce options available which allow you to set up shop online without having to invest in expensive hardware and software. Generally you will have to take care of delivering the goods to your queues of eager customers, so factor that work into your calculations. There are some services which handle this for you too – see next page.

Where do I start?

What do you want to do? Books? T-shirts? Computer paraphernalia? Try to think what will work best for your audience, then do some research into companies which produce that kind of product. What do these products cost at the point of sale, and what are the production costs? Look at your traffic stats and work out how many units you might sell if 1% of your regular readers bought one. What about 0.1%? Having bought one, will they ever need to buy another? Now bear in mind that it may turn out to be an inexplicable but total disaster. Work out how much cold hard cash you are prepared to risk – and how much blood, sweat and tears you are prepared to shed – to shift what may only be a dozen mouse mats.

If the answer to the cold hard cash question is 'none', take a look at CaféPress (www.cafepress.com). This is an online marketplace which offers print-on-demand production of all manner of merchandise, a 'shop' on their site to sell them from, and handles all of the order management and customer service for you. All you have to do is send in the designs, so you are

looking at zero investment and zero ongoing costs. Of course you pay a price for this – not up-front, but they will take a decent cut out of the retail price – so you need to weigh up your appetite for risk against reward and decide which approach is best for you.

And finally ...

Before you do any of this, take a good hard look at whether your money-spinning idea stands a real chance of working for you – you may not have to invest a lot of money in starting up a collection of tacky mugs and baseball caps, but will people really buy them? How will they find out about them? The bedrock of any blog-related revenue scheme is a good, popular weblog. If you're not already pulling in a solid, loyal audience, put down the coloured pens and fabric swatches and get back to the blog! Being an entrepreneur is about taking risks, yes, but it is also about knowing when to focus on your core business – your blog. Make it the best blog it can be – blog because you love it, because you have something you want to say – and everything else will follow.

Summary

- Join an ad network to make the most effective use of advertising on your blog.

- Find out what your blogging service offers – some will have their own ad schemes which you can join very easily.

- Keep your expectations realistic about making money from a blog.

- Be creative and take the initiative on merchandising, books and audio or data CDs.

- Love your weblog! And the money will follow (maybe).

taking it further

In this chapter you will learn:

- about various blogging services available

- about some well-known blogs

- where to find further sources of help online

12.1 What services are out there?

In this book we've concentrated on the two biggest hosted services out there: Blogger and TypePad. There are a number of other notable blogging tools and hosted services which are very blog-like. As the popularity of blogs and social software on the Web grows, so new services enter the market on a regular basis. By the time you read this, there may be a number of important new systems online, but here are a few of the significant ones at the time of writing.

12.2 Blogging tools

WordPress

http://wordpress.org/ or http://wordpress.com

WordPress is a powerful, open-source (i.e. free to use) piece of weblogging software which can be installed on a host server or hosted for you at WordPress.com. A purist's approach to weblogging and the developers have made an honest product and service with a lot of integrity. Might be a bit geeky and

WordPress.com is the hosted service using the WordPress software

involved for the novice user, but definitely worth checking out if you're interested in supporting an open-source project.

Expression Engine

http://www.pmachine.com/

This is a publishing tool that can support quite sophisticated web publishing at the top end, but it is also useful as a blogging system for intermediate level users. It's a software solution only; you'll need to hook up a hosting service provider to get your site online. The same company, PMachine, offers a hosting solution that integrates nicely with the ExpressionEngine software – find this at http://www.pmachinehosting.com. A range of licences in the software and packages on the hosting are available, depending on your intended use.

ExpressionEngine from PMachine

Blogware

http://home.blogware.com/

Blogware is a wholesale weblog service from online services wholesaler, Tucows. It's a browser-based publishing system, so there's no need to download any software. You buy the service from a number of resellers, and it's possible to sign-up with Tucows to become a Blogware reseller yourself.

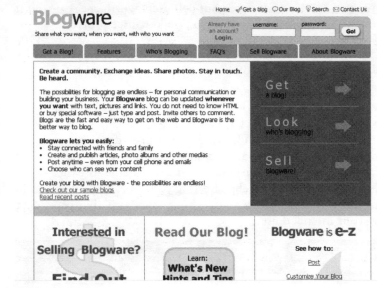

Wholesale blogs from Blogware

UserLand

http://www.userland.com

One of the original weblog software and service providers, UserLand offer two software products; Manila and Radio

Radio UserLand is one of the original and still popular weblogging services

UserLand. The latter is the entry level product, supporting personal and small business type weblogs with hosting and server space offered as part of the service. Manila is the more powerful enterprise level, server-based solution, with lots of features for sharing information with colleagues, across projects.

12.3 Blog-like communities

LiveJournal

http://www.livejournal.com/

LiveJournal was one of the first social networking sites and in 2005 was acquired by Six Apart, the same company who offer the TypePad service. It offers a mix of personal publishing of text and pictures 'journals' but also offers the ability to create and join communities, which are collectively authored sites within LiveJournal on every topic under the sun.

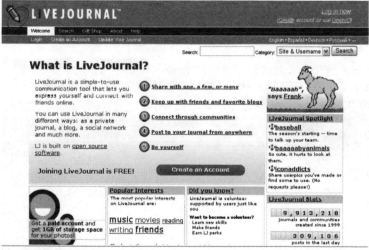

LiveJournal is a super community site owned by the people who brought you TypePad

MySpace

http://myspace.com/

In 2005 this community of personal web pages was acquired by Rupert Murdoch's News Corporation and marked a significant step towards the mainstream media's acceptance of online social networking as an integral part of its strategy. In MySpace the emphasis is on creating a personal profile and then using that presence in the community to talk with old friends or make new ones. As part of its offer it does support blogging and commenting, plus a range of multiple media and is free to use.

Even Rupert Murdoch's into personal publishing now with News Corp's acquisition of MySpace

MSNSpaces could be a good place for junior bloggers to start

MSNSpaces

http://spaces.msn.com/

This is Microsoft Network's weblogging and personal publishing service. If you already have a Microsoft Passport login for Hotmail or Messenger, then it is very easy to create your space on the Network. It offers some blogging functionality and a lot of tools to manage access to pages which may make this a very safe learner's tool, especially for junior bloggers.

12.4 Some A-list blogs

Boing Boing

http://www.boingboing.net

One of the most visited, highly-regarded weblogs, Boing Boing is the collective work of Cory Doctorow, Mark Frauenfelder, David Pescovitz, Xeni Jardin and John Battelle. It talks about technology and entertainment plus anything else it feels like, with bags of attitude and not a little humour. Be one of the 17 million who visit every day.

suggest a link | defeat censorware | rss | archives | store | mark | cory | david | xeni | john

[   ] Search Boing Boing

THURSDAY, APRIL 13, 2006

Are phony photos in a MySpace profile "ID theft"?
Bill Poon, a blogger who lives in Los Angeles, says was fired from his day job for posting a photo in his own personal MySpace profile -- a photo of the president of the company where he worked. Bill says he didn't disclose the name of the company or disparage its prez, and says he only posted the image for one week as a friendly joke for co-workers. What makes the story interesting, though, is the fact that the manager who fired Bill described the act as "identify theft," and "a criminal offense," and threatened legal action:

> I put it up for a week and left comments for co-workers saying "go back to work" and "good job". Apparently, the humor was lost on the "counsel" (I'm rather flattered that the fate of a lowly burgermaker like me would be determined by a "counsel" I guess my burgers are that damn good) and said that the only recourse was

Boing Boing, possibly the world's most popular blog

Gawker

http://www.gawker.com/

Gawker is the hip and bitchy work of Jessica Coen and Jesse Oxfeld tracking the comings and goings of media figures in Manhattan and obsessing about everything from Teri Hatcher to Donald Rumsfeld, reporting from what they term the 'centre of the universe'.

Gawker, the hip and bitchy work of Jessica Coen and Jesse Oxfeld

The Diary of Samuel Pepys

http://www.pepysdiary.com/

This is an ingenious use of the weblog form to re-present the work of the seventeenth century, proto-blogger, Samuel Pepys. It's a fascinating way to consume one of the greatest pieces of social and personal history in English. This is a labour of love by British web genius Phil Gyford, who has built a vibrant and lively community around the revitalized works of a legendary Londoner.

The Diary of Samuel Pepys

The diary | Background info | Recent annotations | About this site

Diary archive | Introduction | The story so far | RSS/XML

Search: [   ] Go Help

First time here? Read the story so far

Sunday 29 March 1663

(Lord's day). Waked as I used to do betimes, but being Sunday and very cold I lay long, it raining and snowing very hard, which I did never think it would have done any more this year. Up and to church, home to dinner. After dinner in comes Mr. Moore, and sat and talked with us a good while; among other things telling me, that [neither] my Lord nor he are under apprehensions of the late discourse in the House of Commons, concerning resumption of Crowne lands, which I am very glad of. He being gone, up to my chamber, where my wife and Ashwell and I all the afternoon talking and laughing, and by and by I a while to my office, reading over some papers which I found in my man William's chest of drawers, among others some old precedents concerning the practice of this office heretofore, which I am glad to find and shall make use of, among others an oath, which the Principal Officers were bound to swear at their entrance into their offices, which I would be glad were in use still. So home and fell hard to make up my monthly accounts, letting my family go to bed after prayers. I staid up long, and find myself, as I think, fully worth 670l.. So with good comfort to bed, finding that though it be but little, yet I do get ground every

Background info:
Art and Literature
Entertainment
Fashion
Food and Drink
Further reading
General reference
Glossary
Government and Law
Holidays and Events
Money and Business
People
Places
Religion
Science, Technology, Health
Travel and Vehicles
Work and Education

Pepys diary, seventeenth-century words in a twenty-first century package

Engadget

http://www.engadget.com/

The world's leading gadget blog, this reads like the catalog from an electronics retailer in the far future. Engadget is full of news and reviews of new products and features a weekly podcast and a very well developed outreach program which organizes readers into local meetings chaired by gadget-loving gurus.

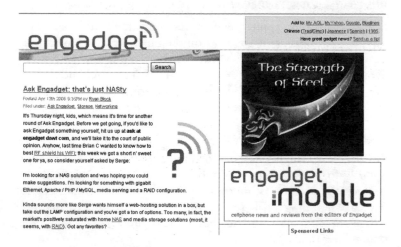

Doc Searls

http://doc.weblogs.com/

Insights and observations from a writer and leading theorist on the importance of blogs in marketing and public relations. Doc Searls is most well-known for writing an influential book on the Internet's impact on marketing, *The Cluetrain Manifesto*. Check his blog for news and tips on technology, marketing and publishing.

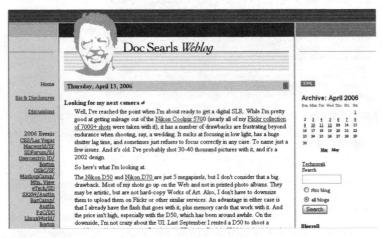

Wonderland

http://crystaltips.typepad.com

Idiosyncratic blog about video games and game culture by Alice Taylor, Jen Bolton and Jez. Lots on the business of video games, new developments and insider gossip from the industry. Wonderland also features crazier bits of game merchandise and personal asides from the lives of its contributors.

PostSecret

http://postsecret.blogspot.com/

PostSecret was highly garlanded at the 2006 Bloggies, the annual awards for great blogs. It's more of a multiple authored art project, the premise being that you should send in a handmade postcard detailing a true secret you've never revealed to anyone. These are scanned in and posted by the organizers and make for compelling reading.

Wonderland – the crazy games world of Alice, Jen and Jez

PostSecret – compelling reading

Scobleizer

http://scobleizer.wordpress.com/

Self-deprecating, Microsoft insider views from Robert Scoble, proclaimed 'technical evangelist'. Scoble's blog is a wide-ranging dragnet on software, computing and blogging but is highly readable and personable for all that. Scoble is also an author of a great book on blogging: *Naked Conversations*.

Scobleizer

April 9, 2006

Blog break time
Munir Umrani asks "where is Mini?"

Heh, I bet someone got him an Xbox! 😊

But, tonight I was talking with Steve Gillmor and told him I was thinking of taking some time off. I've been thinking about this for a couple of weeks now but I wanted to do it with some thought first.

Along these lines Udo Schroeter wonders whether we are just ganging up on people and is that a good "conversation?"

That's what Steve Gillmor and I talked about too.

I'm gonna take some time off, think more about what I want to do as a blogger, as an employee, as a husband, as a father, and come back fresh.

Translation: I gotta play some Xbox! 😊 (Thanks to Chris Pirillo, I didn't know he was gonna video me at brunch today).

I also have a bunch of Channel 9 tasks to do too, I'm way behind there too.

Buy from Amazon

Naked Conversations
Robert Scoble
Best Price $12.47
or Buy New $15.72

Privacy Information

Buy from
Barnes and Noble:

Robert Scoble gets upfront, personal and fascinating

12.5 More help online

There is a huge amount of resources online for all matters relating to blogging. Definitely try your favourite search engine for blogging terms if you get stuck. Here are a few sites that we've found helpful getting this book together.

Blogger Help
http://help.blogger.com/

TypePad Help
http://help.typepad.com/

While these two sites exist to provide help on using their respective systems, they also contain articles on general blogging matters which are helpful whichever blog system you use.

Wikipedia
http://en.wikipedia.org/wiki/Blogging

Massive amount of information on a wide range of blogging topics contributed by volunteers to the Wikipedia project.

Online Journalism Review
http://www.ojr.org/

Thoughtful news and views site reflecting trends and stories that should be of interest to bloggers.

Legal

Electronic Frontier Foundation
http://www.eff.org/bloggers/lg/

The peerless resource for legal pointers and online, free-speech lobbying.

Blogging tools

Blog Rolling
http://www.blogrolling.com/

Weblog Compendium
http://www.lights.com/weblogs/tools.html

Blogging guides

Weblogs
http://www.weblogs.com/

Technorati
http://www.technorati.com/

Kinja
http://www.kinja.com/

Bloggie Awards
http://www.bloggies.com/

These are some of the most popular guides to recently updated, most popular blogs so you can discover new gems in the blogosphere and maybe see your own site listed there.

index